THE STATE AND
THE TRADE UNIONS

By

D. F. MACDONALD

M

OR G.1093.

First edition 1960
Second edition 1976

Published by
THE MACMILLAN PRESS LTD
London and Basingstoke
Associated companies in New York
Dublin Melbourne Johannesburg and Madras

SBN 333 21196 0 (hardcover)
SBN 333 21197 9 (paperback)

Printed in Great Britain by
REDWOOD BURN LIMITED
Trowbridge & Esher

CONTENTS

PREFACE TO THE FIRST EDITION

I HAVE acknowledged in references those sources of fact and opinion on which I have directly drawn, but there are others, both written and oral, which over the years have contributed towards my judgments, such as they are. I owe special thanks to my colleague, Dr. J. T. Ward, who read the typescript and made many useful criticisms; to Mr. J. P. P. Smith; to the publishers' readers, who drew my attention to various faults; and to the publishers themselves, for their interest in the project. It is doubtful if the work would have reached book-form without the help of my wife, who deciphered and typed the manuscript.

Queen's College, Dundee
University of St. Andrews

PREFACE TO THE SECOND EDITION

THE first edition, which appeared in 1960, ended with a chapter entitled 'Past, Present and Future'. The observations in it have since been overtaken by the rapid and dramatic sequence of events, and I have therefore substituted a completely new chapter to bring the narrative up to date.

I again owe a special debt of gratitude to Professor John Ward of the University of Strathclyde for reading and making valuable suggestions on the draft, and to Mrs. Jessie Young for the skill and patience with which she dealt with the preparation of the typescript.

D. F. MACDONALD

CHAPTER I

LABOUR UNDER STATE CONTROL

It would be impossible to mark the starting-point in time of the process by which the State began to take a controlling interest in labour, regarded as a separate element in the national economy, and not as a collection of individuals fused into the community as a whole. Two factors, however, would clearly be involved in the development, the first constitutional, and the second social.

First, there would be the emergence of the State itself as the embodiment of national government, with a central authority wishful and capable of exerting its influence over all activities which it considered to be of national concern. In regard to labour, this would at first sight appear a fairly obvious and simple matter, since, when the State as defined was taking shape, labour and its activities were still in a rudimentary stage, and easily identified. There were, however, traditional restraints on government, which retarded the evolution or implementation of an overall policy. The monarchical State had its roots in feudalism, which was essentially local in character, and which therefore was resistant to the encroachment of central authority. This resistance steadily diminished before the impact of national government, but the Government only slowly acquired the machinery to make effective its decrees. Thus, during the period when labour was emerging as a distinct department of society, the central Government was essentially autocratic; but it had to rely for the execution of its policies largely on local semi-independent agencies in the absence of a comprehensive state bureaucracy.

In the mediaeval State, not only the administration but the whole concept of life was local. Communities, whether villages

I

or towns, were small and in general self-sufficient. The peasant was bound to his lord, the apprentice to his master, and all of them were bound by the rules of the small society of which they were a part, as the bee is part of the hive.

Yet there was one fundamental thing which marked the mediaeval community, and which bridged, however precariously, the division between it and the 'modern' State. It was the conviction that society, whatever its size, was an aggregation of individuals and activities which must work together for the common good. All persons not merely had the right to work, but they were in duty bound to do so, if they were able-bodied, in their appropriate vocations; and a due balance must be preserved between the vocations. All must work honestly and produce honest goods, for sale at an honest price, for otherwise the community would be defrauded. Self-interest was, of course, an ingredient, but, ideally, it was closely regulated on behalf of community-interest. Exploitation by one individual of another or of the group, whether by selling his commodities (including labour) too dear, or by selling those of inferior quality, was abhorrent to the mediaeval morality. That this canon was not universally observed is quite immaterial in the present context; it did represent a doctrine which was at the basis of mediaeval society, and which stubbornly persisted after that society was in the way to decay. It was a doctrine which it was presumed any government, whether local or national, would seek to enforce, and this made interference by Government in all kinds of social and economic activity not only possible, so far as its resources would permit, but to be taken for granted.

The second factor was the recognition — grudging recognition — that labour, and its employers, were beginning to constitute a separate order, with interests and ambitions at variance with those of the community as a whole. In the mediaeval society there were masters employing journeymen and apprentices, a régime by no means ideal from the workers' point of view, but with its asperities somewhat mitigated by the comparative lowness of the class barrier. The industrious apprentice could look forward to acquiring the relatively insignificant capital necessary to set him up in business. Then came almost imperceptibly the beginning of the slow disintegration of this system. It came with the use of machinery and the expansion of the commodity-market, which necessitated the use of capital on an increasing scale. With this came a heightening of the barrier between master and man, both socially and economically. The man became more and more a hired servant, using the master's machines and raw materials, and receiving in return a financial reward. The same process was at work on the land, where the lord, who had had his work done in the form of compulsory service, was obliged by the shortage of labour — to which the great plague in 1348–9 made a particularly strong contribution — to hire men for pay. In short, labour, whether in manufactures or in agriculture, assumed a money value, and the proportion of workers relying for subsistence on the hire of their labour — i.e. wage-earners — grew apace.

It was inevitable that with the loosening of the old economic-social structure, the mediaeval concept of society should become ever more anachronistic. It had deep roots, however, and lived on, in attenuated form, even while modern society was taking shape. The hierarchy of master, journeyman and apprentice continued to be regarded as normal. The central Government took under its wing the old local system of controls, its aim being to prevent the exploitation by the employer of the worker, by the worker of the employer, or by either of the community. For the nation was as vulnerable in its way as the parish had been. It was a rather larger microcosm, an entity dependent for its survival on its own production of food and other basic commodities, so agriculture, manufacture and trade had to be closely supervised in the national interest. The State was still a delicate structure, which had for its very life to assuage so far as possible internal stresses and strains, of which there were many deriving from political and economic changes. It had therefore to take a very real and direct interest in the new economic and social phenomena which were manifesting themselves. Its motives were not primarily moral; it was obsessed with the need for security, and security meant stability. Yet the new economic forces were disruptive of the old order of things, and the perennial problem of Government was how far could they be constrained, for it quickly became evident that they could not be wholly repressed.[1]

It has been stated that 'legislation with regard to labour has always been class legislation', and the labour laws of the Tudors have been cited as proof of this.[2] This is to take a very narrow and misleading view. Government was, of course, class government in the sense that parliamentary influence was restricted to a narrow caste, as was membership of the other governmental bodies, but it was to a peculiar degree truly national government. The monarchy, still based on feudalism, consulted only 'prelates and nobles and other learned men'; but Parliament played a secondary rôle in the running of the country's business, and while the monarchy sought at the least its acquiescence, the shape of State policy was dictated by the royal will working through the Privy Council and its instruments. Government was in short highly personal, through the monarchy and its agencies. Indeed, increasingly during and after Elizabeth's reign, the central authority was constantly exercised with the task of keeping the upper classes in a degree of subjection. Vested interests as such, therefore, while often and increasingly able to exert selfish influence, were much less powerful than they would have been — and became — under a type of government in which authority, and especially financial authority, rested with Parliament. Under the Tudors and the early Stuarts, while the workers had no voice whatever in legislation affecting them, neither had employers as such. They were both regarded as 'of the fourth sort of men who do not rule'.[3]

The implication that the legislation was pro-employer and anti-worker would be quite false, except on the doubtful assumption, made by another and more recent writer, that the State must of its nature be pro-employer and anti-labour because it is its function to protect the public — that is, to protect class property.[4] That much of Tudor and Stuart legislation bore heavily on labour there can be no doubt, although the fault was partly in its administration. Yet a fundamental of its design — an extraordinarily comprehensive design — was to protect labour from the economic vagaries and vicissitudes of the times, and, not least, from exploitation by employers who lacked a proper appreciation of what were deemed to be their natural obligations towards their workers.

The laws certainly discounted any idea of labour organising in its own defence. The idea would, at that stage of industrial and social development, have been quite impracticable; but it would in any case have been inconceivable to Government. For workers (or employers) to band themselves together for such a purpose would have been to usurp the functions of the State, whose duty it was to ensure balance and good order in all things. It would have been a sort of organised factional rebellion and, if successful, it would have meant that a section was imposing its will on the rest of the community.

The reign of Elizabeth provides the perfect illustration of State policy towards labour, in this context. Much of her programme was a re-assessment and re-codification of the more piecemeal and extemporised provisions enacted over the previous century and a half, and was embodied in the Statute of Artificers, or, better called, the Statute of Labour (1563).[5]

Its purpose was to make 'one sole law' on the subject of industrial relationships. It was a national law for the generality of industry, replacing previous local and sectional enactments. It was not a law to depress the workers; on the contrary, its chief justification was expressly stated to be that the rates of wages prescribed in previous statutes were too low, having regard to the rise in prices, and could not be enforced 'without the great grief and burden of the poor labourer and hired man'. It was intended that its effect should be to 'yield unto the hired person both in the time of scarcity and in the time of plenty a convenient proportion of wages'. Accordingly, J.P.s, in consultation with other 'grave and discreet persons', were required annually to determine rates of wages — maximum rates, however, with penalties for employers and workers for exceeding them. On the other hand, there was to be elasticity, for the rates were to have due regard to the commodity prices prevailing from time to time. There was, in fact, to be a wages-policy of sorts, related to the idea — it was little more — of a cost-of-living index.

That Government's intention was not to 'freeze' wages was demonstrated later in the reign when an Act was drafted for the textile industry, where the growth of capitalism and the emergence of a wage-earning class were most marked. It realistically attributed poor workmanship to poor remuneration, and insisted not only on a better standard of wages for the future, but on the maintenance of higher rates where these already operated. This trend of thought was given clearer expression in James I's Act of 1604, 'Empowering Justices to Fix Minimum Rates of Payment'. Referring to the Statute of Labour, it forthrightly condemned the failure to make allowance, in wage-fixing, for the cost of living, and stipulated that the rates to be prescribed should be regarded as minimum rates, and that higher rates already prevailing should continue. Employers were liable to penalties for non-compliance, the fine, aptly enough, to go to the aggrieved workman. The Act applied to workers in all industries, as did a similar Act of Charles I (1640).[6]

It is clear that there was a growing recognition of the need to protect workers, particularly the new artisan class. There were other features of the legislation of this period which were less palatable to the workers. Most of the legislation was double-edged, and was meant to be. It restricted free movement of labour by the laws of settlement. It insisted on long-term hirings, which might be onerous to the wage-earner, and were certainly designed to discourage what was seen as unhealthy competition for workers between different industries; but were also to promote continuity of employment. Agriculture, being vital to the economy, was to be ensured an adequate supply of workers by the direction of labour to it. The apprenticeship provisions were harsh; but they did seek to protect the skilled worker against 'dilution of labour', and to maintain reasonable standards of workmanship. The Poor Laws were severe and unimaginative. They were inspired partly by the need to prevent dangerous vagabondage, but their schemes of compulsory employment were not simply penal; they were motivated also by the desire to 'banish idleness' in fulfilment of the creed that work was not only a right but a social obligation. Labour legislation in fact was part of a grand and well-intentioned design to preserve stability, to put the brake on innovation with menacing social implications.

The doctrine of the 'just price' was applied to other basic commodities, as well as labour. The activities of middlemen who 'cornered' supplies of raw materials, 'caring only for their own private gain without having any regard to the maintenance of the commonwealth', were condemned. 'Truck' dealings by employers were forbidden. The use of labour-saving machinery, with its corollary of unemployment, was restricted, and might be prohibited; thus in 1623 the Privy Council authorised the breaking-up of a needle-making machine. In agriculture, too, labour-saving was deprecated, 'that being the best way of tillage which employeth most about it'. Employers were sharply reminded at times of their social responsibilities; they might be compelled to carry on business in times of depression even at a loss, on the grounds that 'those who had gained in profitable times must now be content to lose for the public good until the decay of trade was remedied' — a remarkable doctrine, it might seem, but not at all incongruous in the pattern of the times. In the depression of 1620-4, merchants were commanded to lay in stocks, manufacturers were given a moratorium against their creditors and work programmes were devised for the unemployed. The same depression led to the appointment of the first royal commission to investigate the causes of unemployment.[7]

The good 'maintenance of the commonwealth' was the constant central theme, and the social and economic code laid down was in essence the mediaeval code brought up-to-date and put on a national basis.

It is against this background that the policy towards labour must be viewed. It was an offence for labour to extort unreasonable and excessive wages by exploiting a shortage of workers, as happened when London was being re-built after the Great Fire of 1666. The organisation of labour simply had no place in the scheme of things; combinations of any sort were suspect, since they could have no justification except to intrude on the province of the State, and to fleece the public. On this assumption, Acts against combinations in particular trades had been passed since at latest the beginning of the fourteenth century; an Act of 1303 forbade workers in cord-waining to concert arrangements 'to the prejudice of the trade and the detriment of the common people'.[8]

The policy of state-control can be judged to have had a fair measure of success, having regard to the difficulties in its way. This was a period of expansion and of inflation. Government did not burke the issues raised by these factors. Economists had not yet devised a jargon to disguise inflation, or theories to extenuate it; it was frankly recognised as debasement of the currency. The attempt to control wages and prices was part of the campaign against it, but the enlargement of demand, the growth of trade and the inflow of bullion from overseas made the task almost impossible. So far as wages were concerned, in spite of the elasticity provided for by law, there was an inevitable tendency to renew the existing rates when they came up for review, regardless of the fluctuations in prices, although in practice economic forces were the final determinant. The machinery of administration was weak, since it centred on the J.P.s, who were unpaid and prone to be neglectful of their duties. They were also liable, it was said, to be unduly sympathetic to the interests of employers, although this was not always the case. This weakness was recognised by the central Government, and the Act of 1604, already mentioned, stipulated that cloth manufacturers, being interested parties, were not to act in this capacity for wage-fixing. In the early seventeenth century, their operations were more closely supervised. The central machinery was strengthened — too much so for the taste of the landowners and industrialists. The Star Chamber and the Court of Requests, although they came to be denounced as instruments of autocracy — as indeed they were — were intended for the protection of the weak against the oppressor, and discharged this prime function with striking success. For instance, the Star Chamber imposed a heavy fine and a pillory sentence on a speculator found guilty of engrossing corn. The Court of Requests was known as the 'Court of Poor Men's Causes', because of its reputation for dealing with cases cheaply and swiftly. The system reached its apotheosis under Charles I — significantly enough, when parliamentary government was at a low ebb.[9]

Industry was expanding, but the Crown — that is, the Government — clung to the view that this expansion must be regulated, in its nature and direction. This was to be achieved through the licensing of monopolies, which, so far as they were meant to restrict undesirable competition and to maintain good order in industry, had much in common with the old gilds. Industry and commerce, like labour, were of course not merely to be regulated, but to be protected and fostered. But industry and commerce were becoming strong and self-reliant, and impatient of the shackles that bound them, of the exclusive privileges which inhibited competition, and often put a premium on incompetence and corruption. The abuses of the system were more flagrant than its merits as an agency of paternal State control. In any case, State control (as then understood) was by now anathema to landowners and industrialists, whether it was exercised in economic affairs, or in religious or constitutional matters. The mounting opposition

B

to the Stuarts in England and Scotland was inspired only in part by the fear of religious dictation; it was, in the first place, a revolt by an oligarchy against personal government in all its manifestations. All the dissenting, dissatisfied elements were rallied against a régime which doggedly hung on to its own rigid conceptions of government. The oligarchy was successful, as it was bound to be, for it not only represented a demand for liberty against authoritarianism, but had behind it the most active sections of the power and wealth of the nation.[10]

It is interesting, if profitless, to speculate whether, if the monarchy had been a little more accommodating, more receptive of new ideas, the system of State control could have been maintained in principle, and adapted to changing circumstances. This would in turn have required the building up of an elaborate administrative machinery to give effect to State policy — in fact, the creation of a bureaucracy to implement laws designed to reconcile the various interests concerned in an expanding economy. It would have been at least as natural a development of central government to fashion a civil service in the seventeenth century, as it was two hundred years and more later. The idea and practice of an all-pervasive State intervention already existed, with well-established sanctions; it had to be re-created in the nineteenth century in face of another tradition of freedom from controls. The question is, however, quite unreal. Assuming that the Stuarts had bought the survival of the monarchy at the price of giving parliamentary power to the oligarchy — which was the bargain made in the Revolution — it is inconceivable that the new rulers would long have tolerated a system which restricted freedom of action in the economic sphere.

REFERENCES

1. R. H. TAWNEY: *Religion and the Rise of Capitalism* (Penguin Books, 1938), pp. 70–1 and 154–5;
   E. LIPSON: *The Growth of English Society* (A. & C. Black, 1954), pp. 144–5;
   E. F. HECKSHER: *Mercantilism* (Allen and Unwin, 1935), I, pp. 226–7.
2. W. S. JEVONS: *The State in Relation to Labour* (Macmillan, 1882), pp. 33–4.

3. *Statutes & Constitutional Documents 1558–1625,* ed. G. W. PROTHERO (Oxford, Clarendon Press, 1913), Introdn., pp. lxii, xcviii–xcix, 177.
4. H. J. LASKI: *Trade Unions in the New Society* (Allen & Unwin, 1950), pp. 51–2.
5. *Tudor Constitutional Documents, 1485–1603,* ed. J. R. TANNER (Cambridge University Press, 1922), pp. 502–6.
6. *English Economic History — Select Documents,* ed. BLAND, BROWN & TAWNEY (Bell, 1937), pp. 336–43;

    E. LIPSON: *Economic History of England* (A. & C. Black, 1934), III, pp. 251–7;

    K. KELSALL: *Wage Regulation Under the Statute of Artificers* (Methuen, 1938).
7. D. C. COLEMAN: 'Labour in the English Economy of the Seventeenth Century' (*Economic History Review,* 1955–6), pp. 280–95;

    E. LIPSON: *Economic History of England,* III, pp. 304–10;

    E. F. HECKSHER: (*op. cit.*), pp. 256–7, 264;

    E. LIPSON: *The Growth of English Society,* pp. 247–8.
8. E. F. HECKSHER: I, p. 310;

    W. MILNE-BAILEY: *Trade Unions and the State* (Allen & Unwin, 1934), pp. 167–8;

    E. LIPSON: *Economic History of England,* III, pp. 386–9.
9. E. LIPSON: *Economic History of England,* III, pp. 244–7, 254–6;

    E. F. HECKSHER; I, pp. 250–3, 279.
10. E. F. HECKSHER; I, pp. 295–6;

    E. LIPSON: *Growth of English Society,* pp. 172–6.

CHAPTER II

THE GROWTH OF LABOUR ORGANISATION

THE Restoration restored the monarchy, but one subject to an increasing degree of control by Parliament. It marked the beginning of the end of an ancient conception of government, and the end itself came with the Revolution.

It was not that Parliament set out deliberately to depress the condition of the wage-earners. The bulk of the labour code remained on the statute-book for well over a century; but it became steadily more incongruous in its new setting. The demand that free play should be given to economic forces grew ever more clamant. As the eighteenth century progressed, the view that anything inhibiting the commercial motive, anything 'in restraint of trade', was contrary to the public weal, as interpreted by those in authority, swiftly won ever more adherents, and by the dawn of the nineteenth century there was hardly a politician or an economist to deny it.

It was natural that the commercial interests should maintain it; indeed, in the economic circumstances of the time, the theory of freedom to buy and sell in the best market, to produce as cheaply as possible, was probably correct, so far as the expansion of industry and trade was concerned. It was perhaps to be expected that most employers — and there were notable exceptions — absorbed in pushing new and often precarious enterprises, and obsessed with the profit motive, should regard labour as simply a raw material to be bought at as low a price as possible, and to be treated as a cheap commodity. In this they saw eye to eye with the landlords, with whom the dominance in Parliament rested. The landlords were themselves exploiting new sources of wealth, in the enclosure movement and the improvements in agricultural methods. The value of labour fell, until wages had to be supplemented by poor-relief to provide a subsistence income, and the exodus from the country swelled the manufacturing population.

All in all, it did not seem that labour could expect any succour from either side. Both were at one in their veneration of the rights of private property and private enterprise. The preservation of stability in the social order seemed to the rulers to be the chief end of Government. This outlook did not greatly differ from that of the Tudors and was similarly identified with the preservation of the State. The difference was that the State itself was now identified with an aristocratic class. Socially as well as constitutionally the bulk of the community were of little account. Stability was menaced by change of any kind, since the system was narrow and rigid; it was accordingly cherished by its chief beneficiaries as sacrosanct. Reform was likely to be violent in character, especially in view of the revolutionary doctrines emanating from the Continent. So private interest and political expediency dictated a common policy, to suppress any movement savouring of revolt, whatever its motive. It was an unhealthy climate for any organised movement for the protection of labour.

With this mentality, it was not surprising that the social conscience sank to a new depth of torpor. Again, it was not so much a matter of individual callousness, although this was bred by the segregation of the rich from the rest of society. The working-class was so far removed from the ruling-class that it was difficult for any real sympathy between them to take form. Lack of sympathy went with lack of interest. The lower classes, it was believed, were lower by a natural dispensation; their nature was inferior and their material lot also. They had to be kept in their place, for there resided in them a latent ferocity against the accepted order of society. The French Revolution, it was said, proved this only too clearly, and it behoved a government based on aristocracy to deprive them of any opportunity to vent this ferocity.[1]

The social problems being thrown up by industrialism were in any case hardly recognised as such, except by a few; they were regarded, not as problems, but as the natural phenomena of a vigorous economy. Even if they had been recognised, it would have been in a spirit of frustration, for a cure had not yet been conceived, except in a few enlightened minds. Religion, philosophy and economics furnished ample justifications for in-action. Economic practice was followed, as so often, by economic precept. 'Laissez-faire principles . . . offered a very welcome pretext for doing nothing when nobody knew what to do'. The economists, faithfully reflecting their environment, produced the most convincing arguments in favour of letting prices, in-cluding the price of labour, find their own level under the com-pulsion of economic forces. The very titles of their doctrines — Ricardo's 'Brazen law of wages', Mill's 'Iron law of wages' were indicative of the stress on the theory of unbridled com-petition, and the gospel of supply-demand. Malthus's theory of population was taken as another argument against improving the lot of the lower classes, and therefore encouraging them to be even more prolific. 'Laissez-faire' was much more than an economic doctrine; it was a social philosophy.[2]

Yet Parliament, conservative in all things, was slow to aban-don the old protective legislation. Wages continued to be fixed locally in the eighteenth century, but in ever fewer cases, and mostly in country districts. The rates fixed had little regard to realities, and little or no attempt was made to enforce them. Parliament did not directly discourage the procedure, but it made no attempt to reinforce it against growing neglect, or to introduce new and much needed safeguards for the labouring classes. The other central agencies which had ensured its func-tioning had been swept away or deprived, like the Privy Council, of their authority. The force of inertia still impelled Parliament to discharge its responsibilities when pressed to do so. Bodies of workmen in particular industries, who stubbornly persisted in invoking their rights under the old laws, sent in petitions alleging their abuse, during the eighteenth century, and Parliament mechanically remitted them to committees for investigation and redress. The weavers were hardest hit by the growth of capitalism, and, on the petition of those in the West of England, the Woollen Cloth Weavers' Act of 1756 provided for the fixing of wage-rates by J.P.s; in other words, the Statute of Labour was in this respect re-asserted. Significantly enough, however, this Act was repealed in the following year. As late as 1773, the Spitalfields Act, also designed to protect weavers against exploitation by their employers, was passed, suggesting that Parliament had not yet wholly succumbed to the new economic doctrines. Parliament, however, was growing increasingly impatient of such restrictive policies, and seven years later rejected the weavers' proposal for the institution of a minimum wage as archaic and impracticable. Within Parliament there were still a few champions of a cause already doomed, like Samuel Whitbread, who in 1795 introduced a Bill for the amendment of the Statute of Labour to permit J.P.s to fix minimum wages and hours of agricultural workers. The terms of Pitt, the Chancellor of the Exchequer's, speech in opposition reflected what was now the orthodox view, that labour should be free to sell its wares in the open market (and the Law of Settlement modified accordingly), and that wages should then find their proper competitive level. A similar Bill in 1800 met the same fate. Parliament and other authorities saw little inconsistency between this attitude and a measure of concern over the plight of the depressed workers. It is noteworthy that the Berkshire magistrates, when they evolved their famous Speenhamland scheme of poor relief in 1795, while acknowledging that the old system of wage regulation was no longer 'expedient', 'very earnestly recommend(ed) to the Farmers and others throughout the country to increase the pay of their labourers in proportion to the present price of provisions'.[3]

Unfortunately for labour, it could not effectively combine to defend and promote its interests in a competitive world. Until the end of the eighteenth century, the law did not prohibit combinations as such, but it forbade as conspiracies in restraint of trade combinations, whether of workers or employers, to determine wages and other working conditions, since in theory this remained the prerogative of the State. There was nothing to prevent workers combining, as the weavers did, to seek parliamentary action on their behalf, or to secure the enforcement through the courts of the existing moribund laws. There were in fact many combinations in existence by the end of the eighteenth century, without molestation from courts or employers. Many employers were themselves harassed, like their workers, by the inroads of capitalism and competition, and they had a good deal of sympathy with the workers' aims, at least so far as they were directed to the establishment of certain minimum common standards. Indeed, there were those who were not above inciting strikes, and even subsidising them, to this end.

Generally the combinations were confined to the superior artisan class, who saw their traditional status and privileges as craftsmen eroded by capitalism, and they were most common in the old-established centres of industry. They did not represent a reaction of the down-trodden masses against exploitation. Their organisation, methods and aims were primitive, which accounted for much of the distrust they inspired in official quarters. They sought, in particular, to impede the introduction of new machinery, and to enforce out-of-date regulations in regard to apprenticeship.[4] They fought a battle which they were bound to lose, regardless of the law.

Combinations were liable to prosecution under statute or common law either because in their objects they trespassed on territory covered by the State, or on the more indiscriminate and nebulous charge that they were 'conspiracies in restraint of trade'. The right to 'free course of trade' was of ancient origin; it applied equally to labour and capital, and any violation of it was an offence, on the grounds that a 'combination of many, to do a wrong, in a matter where the public has an interest, is a substantive offence of conspiracy'.[5] This justification for attack had been increasingly resorted to in the seventeenth

and eighteenth centuries, although regarded askance by some
jurists. The courts reflected the dislike of combinations, especially in the eighteenth century, by interpreting the common law
to repress them. Even when combinations were illegal, the
position was that they were merely outside the law, and positive
action against them was by the private promotion of a Bill at
the instance of an interested party, directed against the objectionable practices of an individual combination. There were
forty such Acts by the end of the eighteenth century, which is a
measure of the prevalence of labour organisations of one kind
or another. It should, however, be noted that Acts of this sort
generally purported to make provision for fixing wages, thus
maintaining the theory of statutory control. The Bill against
combinations of journeymen millwrights, which gave the cue for
the Combination Act of 1799, also enabled magistrates to regulate their wages. The machinery of the Acts was obviously much
too cumbrous to provide an effective deterrent to combinations,
which were usually temporary in purpose and character.[6]

Adam Smith argued that there were 'no Acts of Parliament
against combining to lower the price of work, but many against
combining to raise it'. This was true, but the situation was not
simply or mainly the reflection of a capitalist bias on the part of
Government, as is often suggested; rather was it the outcome of
the constitutional procedure for promoting legislation through
private bills, which rich and influential employers could exploit
for their own ends. Parliament and the law frowned on combinations of any sort, including associations of employers to
raise prices.

The notorious Combination Act of 1799 marked a new departure. It was directed against all illegal combinations — not,
it should be observed, against combinations as such. No doubt
its sponsors were inspired partly by the fear of subversive organisations which might incubate in Britain the germs of the French
Revolution, although, ironically enough, the Revolutionary
Governments in France in 1789 and 1791 prohibited trade
unions and forbade strikes. Trade unions were not immune

from the contagion, since drastic constitutional change or out-right revolution seemed to many of their members to offer the only hope of a solution of their sore grievances. The Government, alert to any sign of sedition, saw them in this light. In part, the law was due to the dislike of trade unions as such, which was not confined to reactionaries; for instance, Wilberforce was a notable champion of reform, but it was he who had suggested that the law should be extended against combinations, which he considered 'a general disease in our society'.

The Act did not really represent any sudden, reactionary shift in State policy; it was an almost fortuitous widening of the existing policy's application, for it seems to have come about more by chance than by deliberate planning. What happened was that yet one more bill in respect of a single occupation was, on the initiative of Wilberforce and Pitt, enlarged into a general Act. It was not designed to be more punitive than the existing laws but rather to speed up procedure. It was becoming obvious, too, that the laborious piecemeal approach hitherto followed was not well adapted to a problem growing in size and intensity so rapidly.[7]

The Act forbade the association of workers for industrial action, including fixing of wages and hours. There were in Parliament, as outside it, people who disliked it, such as Benjamin Hobhouse and Sheridan, in the House of Commons, and Lord Holland — not because they favoured trade unions, but because they thought the procedure prescribed by the Act iniquitous, or believed that the existing legislation was adequate. The campaign against it was so strong as to produce the amended Act of 1800, which went through without any opposition. This, while retaining the prohibition of combinations, considerably improved the procedure, and faintly echoed the old doctrine of parliamentary responsibility, by not only providing for arbitration in disputes, but prescribing penalties for refusal to accept arbitration. For the first time, too, the prohibition of combinations expressly included those of employers to reduce wages or increase hours or the quantity of work, which showed that Parliament remained hostile to combinations of every sort; in other words, it still adhered to the theory that the issues involved were the business of the State.[8] In this, as in other aspects of government, it displayed unresponsiveness to the new forces at work in the country. Paradoxically enough, at the same time it demonstrated, in regard to labour, that it was not merely paying lip-service to an outworn dogma, by tentatively addressing itself to the social problems of industrialisation, in passing the Health and Morals of Apprentices Act (1802), the first in the long series of Factory Laws.

The effect of the Combination Act on trade unions has been exaggerated. Within a few years it was said to be 'a dead letter'. It could be, and was, harshly applied; but it was less tyrannical and less effective than action under the common law. Successful prosecutions under it seem to have been comparatively few in number, and altogether it was 'a negligible instrument of oppression'. Employers, who must initiate prosecution, were generally reluctant or fearful to do so. The expense of court actions was considerable, and the courts were not disposed as a rule to be sympathetic to the employers' case. Magistrates apparently did not care to be involved in disputes between masters and workmen. Masters, too, hesitated to challenge combinations, which were often surprisingly powerful, having regard to their legal position. For instance, in Manchester, the engineers' union controlled the supply of labour, including the intake of apprentices. Protracted strikes took place, without any attempt to invoke the law against them.[9]

The Act was most commonly used in the case of the textile industry, where the factory system was growing apace, and the opportunities for trade unionism were correspondingly great. The trade unions' methods invited and even provoked attack. Partly, no doubt, as a result of repression, those in the factory trades were liable to have a furtive, unsavoury character, with secret rites and seditious aims. Their methods were savage; machine-smashing, physical violence, even murder, were weapons in the fight against employers as unscrupulous and

brutal in their own way — who also formed illegal combinations — and against non-union men. Yet many combinations
survived, in some cases with the connivance of employers, and
some were flourishing, and well organised; these were confined
to the craftsman class. Collective bargaining over wages and
conditions was not uncommon.

It could be held that the most unfortunate thing about the
Combination Acts was that in effect they established the principle that Parliament should attempt to regulate industrial relations — that is, the conduct of workers and employers as such
towards each other — by 'exceptional legislation', instead of
leaving them to be governed indirectly by the ordinary laws
covering citizens in general. The State thus committed itself to
a course of the utmost delicacy and intricacy, in which it had
to attempt to reconcile the conflicting aspirations of masters
and workmen as two distinct classes, and at the same time safeguard the interests of the individual and the community. It was
an almost impossible task.

The Acts did not end the authority of J.P.s to fix wages, and
wage-assessments were made at least as late as 1801. The wage-
clauses of the Statute of Labour were repealed in 1813, and the
apprenticeship clauses in 1814. There was little enthusiasm in
or out of Parliament for labour legislation, the reformers con-
centrating at this time on constitutional change as the means of
progress. The impetus for abrogation of the penal laws came
from those who believed in 'laissez-faire', and thought it should
extend to freedom to combine, so long as that right was not
used to coerce either the community or the individual. Indeed,
Francis Place, who was of the Benthamite persuasion, began
his agitation for repeal of the Combination Laws not with the
aim of encouraging trade unionism, but in the conviction that
the movement, with all its crudity and violence, was fostered by
the Laws and that, with the removal of persecution, trade unions
would cease to have reason for existence. Employers were by no
means wholly for repressive legislation; some of them gave
evidence in favour of its removal when at last a Committee of

the House of Commons was appointed to investigate the question. Influential organs of the press, such as *The Scotsman*, were sympathetic. The Committee was impressed by the arguments, and by the contrast between the restrictions on trade unions of workers and the freedom in practice of employers' associations, and it recommended the repeal of the Act, amendment of the common law, and provision for arbitration (a device which was already being used to good purpose), while condemning any attempt by workers or employers to 'interfere with that perfect freedom which ought to be allowed to each party of employing his labour or capital in the manner he thought best'. It agreed, too, that masters and workmen's associations should be treated alike.

Parliament accepted the recommendation, and the repealing Act was passed in 1824 without debate. Its easy passage through both Houses is alleged to have been due to the preoccupation with other affairs of members hostile to the trade unions, and certainly it was adroitly piloted, so that the Prime Minister could later insist that he had not been aware of it. On the other hand, the issues had been fully ventilated. The Committee had been appointed, as Huskisson said, to give Parliament leisure and opportunity to consider the issues involved, and its findings had been quite unequivocal. That there was hostility to trade unions there can be no doubt, but the long freeze of the eighteenth century was slowly thawing and a reforming movement was gradually gaining strength. The Act, even if passed in haste — as indeed was the Combination Act it revoked — certainly reflected a genuine belief, both in and out of Parliament, that repression, in this as in other directions, was overdone, that the Act was a useless irritant, and that the time was ripe for a relaxation of the law. If wage-earners, said John Bright — an ardent reformer, but no friend of trade unions — were to be regarded as 'a separate and suspected order in our social system', they were bound to constitute a revolutionary element. The sponsors of the Bill certainly hoped that repeal would end trade union violence, if not trade unionism.[10]

The Act of 1824 was surprisingly liberal for the times. It did much more than merely repeal the Combination Acts; it also removed combinations as defined — and the definition was remarkably wide — from the reach of the law, including the oppressive common law of conspiracy. They were no longer to be 'liable to any indictment or prosecution for conspiracy or to any other criminal information or punishment whatever under the common or statute law'. Strikes and lock-outs were specifically sanctioned. The Act covered combinations of men and of masters.

This was a generous approach, whatever the motives. Trade union history might well have followed different channels, and assumed a different character from what it in fact did, if the Act had been left on the statute-book. There would have been much less sense of grievance and class-consciousness, and unions might have fitted more easily and naturally into the pattern of community-growth. The Act would almost certainly have been left to operate quietly and to take root but for one thing; so far from its making for good order, it released a spate of combinations, often of the most irresponsible kind, and an outburst of industrial unrest, signalised by outrageous demands and physical violence to the point of murder. The trade unions, said Hume, who had introduced the Act, were 'estranging their best friends'.[11]

This made inevitable an amending Act (1825) of a much stricter character. Even so, it marked a great step forward. Place himself apparently thought the fundamentals of the previous Act had been preserved. The right of combination remained, but now it was again made subject to the common law in regard to conspiracies in restraint of trade, unless the functions exercised were within the narrow limitations of the Act. These limitations allowed trade unions to deal only with questions of wages and hours, while the right to strike or lock-out in this narrow context was implied, subject to new safeguards against intimidation.

It is an expression both of the attitude of the legislators and of the nature of the problem before them as they saw it in its essentials, that the purpose of the Act was 'to make further provision as well for the security and personal freedom of individual workmen in the disposal of their skill and labour, as for the security of the property and persons of masters and employers'. On the face of it, this was a reasonable aim, and Parliament should not be called reactionary or cynical or short-sighted because it failed to meet the dilemma of reconciling the corporate freedom of associations with the individual freedom of workers and employers; later legislators with more experience and sympathy were to fail in this. Parliament was resolved to prevent violence, not only against the rights of property, but against the individual conscience, which the Act of 1824 had, on the evidence, failed to do. In this its members were at one with their eighteenth century predecessors, who were also activated by the belief that 'the chief, though not the sole duty of the State is to protect men's persons and property, so as to secure the maximum of freedom for each man compatible with the existence of the like freedom on the part of others'.[12] The ban on intimidation derived from this doctrine. On the other hand, Parliament did now make a forward move, in accepting the fact that economic circumstances justified associations of workers and employers in pursuit of their respective legitimate interests.

Those interests, it is true, were narrowly defined. There was, however, no cause to believe at this time that this restrictive qualification was unreasonable, or that it would prove unduly irksome. The greatest defect in the Act was that combinations continued to be exposed to the vagaries of the common law, as interpreted by judges in the light of their personal views of what constituted 'conspiracy'. It was not likely that judges, reflecting, as they often did, the social prejudices of their time, and in particular the bias towards individualism, would be lenient in such cases; and, in fact, after 1825 the common law was invoked against trade unions to an unprecedented extent. Nevertheless, practices which were not expressly permitted by the Act continued to be condoned by the courts. Thus, in 1843, a judgment held that 'for a union honestly and peaceably to persuade the working-classes to cease work for the purpose of obtaining the charter is not in itself criminal'. When decisions to the contrary were made in 1851, Parliament was moved to pass the Molestation of Workmen Act (1859), which clearly affirmed the right to strike, and that of peaceful persuasion, for legitimate union objectives.[13]

As stated, the only function which was thought to be the proper province of trade unions was the improvement of wages and hours of work. The unions had pursued other activities, and were to pursue them in the future, for instance the restriction of the supply of labour, but it was hardly to be expected at this juncture that these should be expressly sanctioned by Parliament; nor could Parliament foresee, even if it had tried, that unions would extend their activities far beyond the mere defence of their members' most elementary rights vis-à-vis their employers.

'The surprising thing,' says a modern commentator, 'seems to be that restrictions on combinations were removed so much earlier in this country than in any other, and that the removal should have been substantially maintained even after the outburst of strikes and violence which followed the repealing Act of 1824.'[14]

Neither the limitations of the Act nor the common law doctrine of conspiracy were used to a damaging extent against trade unions, even when they exceeded their legal functions. For a union to be declared illegal usually meant only that the courts would not enforce its agreements, which unions did not regard as a hardship. 'They might be unlawful at common law, but not criminal, only lacking legal rights'.[15]

Trade unions in fact made great headway in the years following the Act. There was an increasing measure of acceptance from the public and from employers, the more striking because of the immoderate practices and attitudes of certain of the unions. Thus the Glasgow cotton spinners exerted what was described as 'a reign of terror' over twenty years, organising the burning of mills and killing of blacklegs, until their leaders were brought to trial in 1838, and sentenced to seven years' transportation. Unions were often arrogant to the point of absurdity in their dealings, as when one (the Builders' Union) demanded of the employers the prohibition of machinery, and strike pay for their members. Employers were often equally truculent and intransigent; their response was to debar their workers from joining trade unions, by their signing a pledge ('the document') to this effect.[16]

The unions' pretensions were by no means confined to industrial relations. Even while the Combination Act was in force, a strike in the Glasgow area brought forth a 'Committee of Organisation for forming a Provisional Government', which appealed to all workers throughout Britain and Ireland to proclaim a general strike in order to force a political revolution. In the 1830's, the idea of uniting all workers in one vast union was inspired by the same objective, to bring about, by a general strike, 'a Different Order of Things'. Those grandiose plans were symptomatic of political more than industrial aspirations. The bodies responsible, like the National Association for the Protection of Labour (1830), and the Grand National Consolidated Trades Union of Robert Owen (an employer), were inevitably hollow and ephemeral, and would have collapsed even without the hostility of the Government or the prosecution of the pathetic Tolpuddle Martyrs.[17]

In the 'forties, however, the more responsible elements on both sides began to assert themselves, and a new direction and character were given to trade unionism. The 'new model' unions, typified by the Amalgamated Society of Engineers, set out to consolidate their position, in regard to their membership and to their relations with employers and the community. The members were of the superior artisan class, with a worth-while stake in industry. They stood to lose by its dislocation, and their efforts were therefore bent to improving their conditions of employment, and promoting their security both in and out of

C

work. They were comparatively affluent, in relation to the mass of unskilled workers, and could pay substantial trade union subscriptions. They represented what came to be called disparagingly by their critics 'the aristocracy of labour'.[18]

Critics there were a-plenty as time went on, within labour ranks, for the movement was in a sense conservative. Yet it represented a natural and healthy phase of growth. Before this the unions were ramshackle organisations, diffusing their strength and antagonising the public and Government in attacks on employers and on the system they were rightly held to symbolise. This was no doubt natural, but it was wasteful and unprogressive. Trade unionism might not have survived at all in such a form, and certainly it could not have built up the stable foundations on which it was later to build without the solid, pedestrian work of the 'new modellers'.

The new leaders by no means ceased to be militant. They did not disown strikes, which, at that stage of industrial relations, were often the only way to force the hand of the unco-operative employers; but strikes they regarded as costly even if successful, and disastrous if failures. 'Strikes are to the social world what wars are to politics . . . crimes unless prompted by absolute necessity,' said one of them.[19] This outlook was reinforced by the growing emphasis on friendly society activities, which required the conservation of funds. The betterment of working conditions was to be achieved by strikes when necessary, but as a rule by such methods as restriction of apprenticeship (although this was illegal under the 1825 Act), by opposition to piecework and overtime and by the encouragement of emigration. Collective bargaining progressed, and it was significant that the economist Nassau Senior advised the Government to move not only against the unions, but also against masters who connived at or encouraged them. The 'new model' unions, too, set out to equip themselves to deal efficiently with their affairs, and to educate their members.

There was a marked tendency towards centralisation, and the devolution of control to the executives, which was accentuated by the fact that, as was not surprising in the circumstances, the men who created the highest posts were often dominating characters, with a profound conviction in their mission. Their methods were often arbitrary, and their discipline harsh, but they evoked respect and confidence in their integrity. Perhaps the most important feature of their policy, however, was the great importance they attached to the education of their members, at a time when ordinary schooling was still denied to most of the working-class.

It was clearly Parliament's intention in this period that employers and workers should devise their own machinery of negotiation, with the minimum of statutory interference. In 1856 a House of Commons Committee recommended that voluntary committees of conciliation and arbitration should be encouraged, but bills to this effect were unsuccessful until 1867, when an Act of sorts was passed, which, like previous legislation on similar lines, had little or no direct effect, but helped to create a favourable climate. Trade unions were taking root, but they were still at a critical stage of growth.

The mood of trade unions and employers was largely influenced by the state of trade. Depression dictated militancy, while with prosperity passions abated. In this period, too, political defeatism, which set in after the Reform Act of 1832, turned the workers' thoughts to industrial action. But the 'new model' unionism, of which the Amalgamated Society of Engineers was the prototype, waxed powerful, and was careful to court public sympathy. It was a sign of the changing atmosphere that when this Union's members were locked out in 1852, the public subscribed £4000 to its funds.[20]

The 'new model' unionism accepted current economic doctrines except that by which labour was a commodity to be marketed at the lowest price. It did not aim to overturn society, and erect another run by the workers. It had a vested interest in peaceful progress, and its aims were to be achieved by collective bargaining and, where necessary, by Parliamentary processes. In both aims it could collaborate with liberal

28   THE STATE AND THE TRADE UNIONS

employers, led by such men, in and out of Parliament, as
A. J. Mundella.

The emergence of well-organised, large-scale unions naturally
inspired employers to form their counter-associations. The two
parties were often naturally antagonistic, prepared if necessary
to use the weapons of strike and lock-out. For instance, in
1859–60, the building trade employers tried and failed to
smash the Union. There were employers genuinely convinced
that 'workers can only be supported permanently by productive
labour, and productive labour can only be permanently provided out of profits; and profits cannot be made without cheap
labour'.[21] On the whole, however, a more amicable relationship was developing. In 1867 it could be said that 'the offensive
spirit of mastership, which sought to carry everything with a
high hand, and settle all matters without considering the wishes
or interests of the workers, has also greatly softened within the
last few years'.[22] The greater softness did not always extend to
labour organisation, as distinct from labour itself. Yet conciliation processes made headway.

Another contemporary observer and ardent labour prota-
gonist could affirm that 'At no time in the history of labour up
to 1867 had labour leaders stood higher in public estimation,
or were trade unions more free from vituperative attack than in
the autumn of 1866. It almost seemed as if old feuds were to be
forgotten.'[23]

REFERENCES

1. B. WILLIAMS: *The Whig Supremacy, 1714–60* (Oxford, Clarendon Press, 1939), pp, 5–9;
   J. H. PLUMB: *England in the Eighteenth Century* (Penguin Books, 1955), Pt. I, Chapter 1, Pt. II, Chapter 2.
2. E. F. HECKSHER: *op. cit.*, I, p. 472;
   E. LIPSON: *Growth of English Society*, pp. 176–80;
   J. M. KEYNES: *The End of Laissez-Faire* (Hogarth Press, 1926), pp. 5–16.
3. S. and B. WEBB: *History of Trade Unionism* (Longmans, Green, 1956), p. 55;
   E. LIPSON: *Economic History of England*, III, pp. 166–70, 392–409;
   LORD AMULREE: *Industrial Arbitration in Great Britain* (Oxford University Press, 1929), pp. 12–24.

4. S. and B. WEBB: p. 44;
   R. Y. HEDGES and A. WINTERBOTTOM: *The Legal History of Trade Union-ism* (Longmans, Green, 1930), p. 11.
5. SIR W. ERLE: *Memorandum in final Report of Royal Commission on Trade Unions*, 1869.
6. *The Early English Trade Unions*, ed. A. ASPINALL (Batchworth Press, 1949), Introdn., p. ix;
   HEDGES and WINTERBOTTOM: pp. 11–12, 17–18.
7. *Early English Trade Unions*, Introdn., pp. xi–xii;
   M. D. GEORGE: *The Combination Laws Re-Considered* (Economic History, I, 1926–9), pp. 214–28.
8. LORD AMULREE: p. 225;
   HEDGES and WINTERBOTTOM: p. 28.
9. *Early English Trade Unions*, Introdn., pp. xiv–xxii;
   M. D. GEORGE: *op. cit.*
10. W. MILNE-BAILEY: *op. cit.*, p. 29;
    Early English Trade Unions, Introdn., p. xxv;
    S. and B. WEBB: pp. 83, 96, 109;
    HEDGES and WINTERBOTTOM: pp. 23, 35.
11. *Early English Trade Unions*, Introdn., pp. xxviii–xxix;
    M. D. GEORGE;
    S. and B. WEBB: p. 108;
    W. MILNE-BAILEY: p. 180.
12. A. V. DICEY: *Law and Public Opinion in England* (Macmillan, 1914), p. 21.
13. HEDGES and WINTERBOTTOM: pp. 53–59;
    W. MILNE-BAILEY: pp. 29–30;
    SIR F. TILLYARD: *The Worker and the State* (Routledge, 1948), p. 272.
14. M. D. GEORGE:
15. HEDGES and WINTERBOTTOM: p. 60;
    Lord Justice FARWELL: in Osborne v. Amalgamated Society of Railway Servants, 1909 (see Chapter V).
16. S. and B. WEBB: pp. 129–70;
    A. HUTT: *British Trade Unionism* (Lawrence & Wishart, 1952), p. 12;
    E. LIPSON: *Growth of English Society*, p. 404.
17. A. PLUMMER: 'The General Strike During 100 Years' (*Economic History*, I, 1926–9), pp. 184–204.
18. *Labour's Turning-Point*, ed. E. J. HOBSBAWM (Lawrence & Wishart, 1948), Introdn., pp. xvi–xvii. Cf. A. E. MUSSON: *Trade Union and Social History* (Frank Cass: London, 1974) pp. 9–11.
19. W. H. G. ARMYTAGE: *A. J. Mundella* (Benn, 1951), p. 53.
20. S. and B. WEBB: pp. 140, 164–5, 222.
21. *Report of Royal Commission on Trade Unions (1869)*, p. xlix.
22. LUDLOW: *Progress of the Working Class*, quoted in LIPSON: *Growth of English Society*, p. 409.
23. G. HOWELL: *Labour Legislation, Labour Movements and Labour Leaders* (Unwin, 1902), p. 158.

CHAPTER III

THE DEVELOPMENT OF LABOUR LAWS

IT has been said that 'the relation of the State to labour is a question not so much of the direct restraint of the labourer as of the manner in which the State can regard the voluntary and unauthorised legislation of the labourers themselves'.[1] This admirably epitomises the story of the relationship in the last quarter of the nineteenth century.

The solid structure of trade unionism, as it appeared to the unions themselves and to the general public, suddenly manifested ugly faults. In 1866 it was revealed that not all the unions had abandoned the 'barbarous usages of a former time'. The so-called 'Sheffield Outrages' were instances of brutal and systematic intimidation of 'blacklegs' and employers, including deliberate maiming and assassination. It was true that the particular outrages brought to the public notice were confined to a few trades, with an unsavoury reputation in other directions, notably cutlery and brickmaking, in Sheffield and Manchester; but they had a sinister implication for the labour movement, for it appeared that violence of this sort was an accepted feature of the normal policy of the unions concerned. There was an uneasy suspicion, too, that while the searchlight had been focused on one murky cul-de-sac, there might well be others still unilluminated.

Leaders of the respectable trade union movement, genuinely shocked by these revelations, wisely did not try to hush things up, but joined in asking the Government — rather rashly, as some thought — for an inquiry into these happenings. The Government duly appointed a Royal Commission (February, 1867), and must have been a little surprised to find this denounced in labour quarters as 'a pretext to the Government to

suppress the unions or materially to curtail what little liberty
the law had given them'.[2] It went out of its way, to an unprecedented extent, to dispel any such fears, by appointing a
judge, Sir William Erle, known not to be hostile to labour, and
two acknowledged partisans of trade unions, Hughes and Harrison. Union leaders were impressed. Applegarth, leader of the
Carpenters' Union, conceded that there was only one member
of the Royal Commission (Roebuck), 'whose sole object was to
make out a case against the Unions'.[3] The Commission ensured
that trade union representatives should be in constant touch
with its proceedings, and should be encouraged to present their
views. All this marked a new and welcome approach to labour
inquiries. Public opinion was, of course, disturbed by news of
trade union excesses, and the critics of trade unionism saw in
them their own justification; but there is no evidence of hysteria
on the subject either in Parliament or in the more sober organs
of the press.

The unions, however, had ample cause for apprehension, for,
immediately after the setting-up of the Commission, they received another and more severe set-back. The 'new modellers'
owed much to the assumption that, in the enlargement of their
functions beyond those stipulated in the Act of 1825, to embrace friendly society activities, they would enjoy the protection
of the Friendly Societies Act of 1855, including the right to
legal redress against defaulting officials. A court judgment now
(1867) established that this assumption was ill-founded in law.
The Boilermakers' Society took legal action for embezzlement
against a branch treasurer. Not only did the magistrates rule that
trade union funds were not covered by the Friendly Societies Act,
but when the case (Hornby v. Close) came before the Queen's
Bench, it was held by the court that a trade union, being in restraint of trade, had no right to the protection of the courts.

Legally, the decision was not a startling one. The consterna-
tion it caused in labour ranks reflected the extent to which trade
unions had enlarged their original functions and the degree of
security which they had come to assume.

The obvious course for the Government was to let the Royal Commission investigate not only the Outrages, but the issues raised by the judgment, and this it did. Indeed, the Commission's main purpose was 'to inquire into the Organisation and Rules of Trades Unions and other Associations', and secondarily to 'investigate any recent acts of intimidation, outrage or wrong', and suggest improvements. Here lay another reason for trade union uneasiness, for there was a danger that the 'atrocious crimes' which the Commission unearthed might prejudice the Commission, the public and the Government against trade unionism. Labour also feared that, at the best, the slow but steady improvement of relations between organised labour and employers would be seriously retarded by the publicity given to the worst side of unionism.[4]

The larger problem of the unions' status in law was not an easy one, and even the advocates of labour were in something of a dilemma. To adopt the simple and obvious solution and give trade unions the legal status of friendly societies or corporations would, of course, also make them vulnerable in exposing them to actions in the courts. This was a danger which the more far-seeing sympathisers, such as Harrison, clearly appreciated.

Evidence was given to the Commission by trade unions and by employers' associations. The former presented a united front, for there was an instinctive closing of ranks to meet the challenge of events, which led in the following year (1868) to the first Trades Union Congress. The latter seem to have been comparatively few in number, and were essentially defensive in character. It was trade union policy to attack employers individually, which led employers to unite as the need arose to meet the particular emergency, retaliating to the strike with a lock-out of all their workers. Such associations were therefore transient and of course voluntary. Special investigators sent on behalf of the Commission to Sheffield and Manchester confirmed that 'crime and outrage have been the habitual methods of enforcing the trade laws' of the unions, whose object was 'the subjection of both masters and men to the rules of the union, and the destruction of the freedom of labour'. 'Rattening' — that is, taking away tools — was one of the milder methods used against 'blacklegs'. Nearly all trade unions, however, imposed restrictions on the employers as regards the number of apprentices and the working of piecework and overtime, and were therefore, said the Report, in restraint of trade and unlawful. Some, like the Amalgamated Society of Engineers, acted as employment agencies for their members, finding them work in other districts, and paying their fares. This Union professed to have branches in Europe, the colonies, and the United States, and had funds of £140,000. Usually the unions were restricted to 'the superior class of workman', and a five-year apprenticeship was a condition of entry. The subscription might be a shilling per week, with an entrance fee. It was common to refuse to work with non-unionists, and even then the practice of 'sending men to Coventry' prevailed.

The attitude of the union leaders who gave evidence was summarised thus by one of them: 'We look upon employers as men . . . who want to get the greatest profit they can out of their capital, while we want to get the greatest profit we can out of our labour'. Incidentally, the Commissioners were inclined to conclude that unions had not been particularly successful in this aim.

The Majority Report was guarded in its recommendations. As was to be expected, it was much concerned with the proofs of coercion of non-unionists, not only directly, but through their families, and it insisted that workers must be free to dispose of their labour as they thought fit, and equally that employers should be free to find their labour. The law as regards coercion should therefore not be relaxed. It recommended that trade unions should no longer be open to the charge of illegality on the grounds that they were in restraint of trade, and that they should be able to get protection for their funds through registration by the Registrar of Friendly Societies, who could withhold registration only if their rules were objectionable.

Objectionable rules would include limitation on the number of
apprentices, on the use of machinery, on piecework and on the
employment of non-union men. 'Trade' and 'benefit' funds
should be kept separate. It considered strikes 'a very rude
method' of settling disputes, but rejected the idea of compulsory
arbitration, 'since there are no admitted principles of decision
on which the arbitrator may proceed'.

The Minority Report, signed by Hughes and Harrison, and
the Earl of Lichfield, was much more forthright. It wanted the
common law regarding combinations to be 'unequivocally re-
scinded', and demanded that there should be no special laws
for labour, and that offences like intimidation should be dealt
with under the ordinary criminal law. The only condition for
registration of unions, with legal protection for their funds,
should be their freedom from criminal designs. The Minority
Report admitted that violence still characterised the workers
in industries other than those under special scrutiny, notably
mining, but considered that it was insignificant compared with
the state of affairs in the 'twenties and 'thirties, when vitriol-
throwing, incendiarism, machine-breaking and murder were
almost commonplace. Hughes and Harrison emphasised the
peaceful nature of trade union activities in general; over ten
years the Amalgamated Society of Engineers had spent £459,000
in benefits, and only £26,000 on disputes, while the record of
the shipwrights and the glass-workers was even more impressive. They were very anxious that unions should not be
liable to be sued as corporate bodies, and should not be
accountable in law to their members.[5]

It is worth noting, in this connection, that a powerful
masters' association gave evidence in favour of removing legal
disabilities from all voluntary combinations, which should,
however, it was argued, be given a quasi-corporate character,
with power to sue and be sued. It also supported the extension
of courts of conciliation and arbitration.[6]

There were, of course, employers who opposed the granting
of greater freedom to the unions, and would have gladly denied

them recognition of any sort. It is therefore striking to see the testimony of a contemporary labour leader to the way in which employers and workers could co-operate in the promotion of labour legislation. In 1867, household suffrage had been instituted, and the trade unions, through their chief leaders, set out to rally the newly-enfranchised artisans to exert pressure on candidates in the general election of 1868 on behalf of trade union interests. As part of the campaign, wrote the witness, 'nearly every constituency in England and Wales, many in Scotland, and some in Ireland were visited, the special fund for which was mainly contributed by large employers of labour, no conditions being attached as to the advocacy of proper and efficient legislation in favour of trade unions, and the rights of labour generally'.[7]

It was not unusual for employers and union leaders to share the same platform for political and public aims. This common approach was often carried into Parliament itself. Before the Commission's Reports appeared, Parliament willingly took temporary measures, in 1868-9, to safeguard union funds, in an Act of 1868, permitting the prosecution of defaulting officials, and an Act of 1869 allowing civil actions for recovery of funds. It has been said that 'the Liberal Government of that day, and nearly all the members of the House of Commons, were covertly hostile to the very principles of trade unionism'.[8] It is difficult to find grounds for this sweeping statement. In fact, labour had many and sometimes unexpected supporters. The delay in acting on the findings of the Commission, usually instanced as proof of the allegation, was due mainly to the Government's preoccupation with other measures, including some warmly supported by labour.

In 1871 the Bill to amend trade union law was introduced. The only noteworthy speech from the employers' point of view was from Mr. (later Lord) Brassey, the son of a great contractor, who, as on previous occasions, showed himself sympathetic to labour's aspirations.[9] The Bill followed the Majority and Minority Reports in recognising that unions should not be illegal because they were in restraint of trade, but they were to be allowed to register under the Friendly Societies Act if their rules were not criminal, as the Minority Report advocated. Trade union funds were thus given protection. The Government was careful to avoid making unions corporate entities, thereby bringing them and their agreements within the jurisdiction of the courts, and unions were therefore specifically exempted from the Friendly Societies and Companies Acts. Not only agreements governing employment, but also those regarding the sale of goods, were made unenforceable at law, so that employers' associations for regulating prices were also covered.[10] Parliament, however, also took to heart the Majority Report's fears as regards coercion (although the Report had not urged any stiffening of the law, only of its enforcement), and the result was that clauses were included making illegal 'molestation', 'watching and besetting', and other like practices associated with strikes. The Government refused to withdraw these last proposals, in spite of protests, but agreed that they should be the subject of a separate Criminal Law Amendment Act of the same year.

The Trade Union Act of 1871 was the first of a series of attempts to devise statutory safeguards for the trade union movement. It proved to have flaws. 'Perhaps this is not surprising, for when a statute of this kind, which runs counter to the currents of common law, is introduced into the main stream of law, it is impossible to foresee the eddies and cross-currents that will be set up, and which will cause dislocation and violence in unexpected places. This occurred in spite of the cautious and carefully considered language used by Parliament.'[11]

It seemed at the time a very fair and adequate measure. A memorandum sponsored by the T.U.C. acclaimed it as 'a complete charter legalising trade unions. . . . Had the Government done so much and nothing more, they would have been entitled to the gratitude of the working classes for fully and faithfully redeeming the promises they had made.'[12] But to list accepted

methods of putting pressure on non-strikers and employers, and
to rank them as criminal offences under the second Act, was
bitterly resented by the unions, as a withdrawal of rights already conceded by the Act of 1859 (now repealed), and a move
'to strengthen the hands of the capitalists'. It was argued that
violence was not peculiar to workers, and that whether it was
industrial or of any other kind, it was adequately covered by
the ordinary criminal law. There was support for this view from
such authorities as William Harcourt and Brassey.[13] The view
of the Government, on the other hand, as of many individuals,
was that violence or coercion which was the product of collective action, should be regarded differently from violence committed by an individual. The Criminal Law Amendment Act,
it was pointed out, was not directed at trade unions; it represented a change in the general criminal law covering all
persons, whether trade unionists or not. The fact remained that
it had a special significance for trade unions, since it repealed
the Act of 1859 and made illegal certain forms of coercive
action against masters or workmen as conspiracy in restraint of
trade. The most the Government would promise was to recon-
sider the Act in the light of experience.

It was at least understandable, particularly having regard to
the Sheffield Outrages, that the Government should be sensitive
on the question of intimidation by trade unions, directed against
non-union labour or employers. It clung to the view that the
liberty of the individual, as well as the rights of combinations,
must be respected. To define precisely, however, what should
and should not be permitted was difficult, and the terms of the
Act made it a potential weapon in the hands of an aggrieved
employer and a hostile judge. There were numerous prosecutions under the Act, not all successful, and in some cases harsh
sentences resulted, while in others the charges were withdrawn,
or the cases dismissed by the magistrates. The notorious case of
the gas-stokers' strike, in 1872, when harsh prison sentences
were imposed on the leaders, which is often cited as symptomatic of an epidemic of reaction, and as an example of the

oppressive working of the Act, was in fact not dealt with under it. In that case the judge decided that the offences proscribed under it did not exhaust all the grounds of liability for conspiracy under the common law, and that, despite the Act, the defendants were guilty of conspiracy to coerce.[14]

The Government was, however, undeniably embarrassed by the outcome of this particular case. When the matter was raised in the House of Commons in 1873, the Attorney-General frankly acknowledged that the judgment was a novel interpretation of the laws of conspiracy, and raised issues which it was proper Parliament should examine. The Solicitor-General went so far as to reject the judge's interpretation of the law, and the Home Secretary in effect went far to confirm this view by reducing the sentence from twelve months' imprisonment to four.[15] Although the Government contrived to refuse amendment of the Criminal Law Amendment Act, labour took comfort from the fact that William Harcourt, who had raised the gas-stokers' case in the House of Commons, and who, on behalf of the T.U.C., had drafted and introduced a bill bearing on it in 1873, was in that year appointed Solicitor-General. Then came a general election.

Apart from the Criminal Law Amendment Act, on which opinions differed, the Government had, in its legislation, demonstrated its practical sympathy with labour. The Master and Servant Act, 1867, greatly mitigated the harshness of the old law, by which breach of contract by the workman was regarded as a criminal offence punishable by imprisonment. The procedure was greatly improved, and imprisonment confined to cases of serious injury to persons or property. This was later (1875) replaced by a Conservative Government with the Employers and Workmen Act, which made the contract a civil one, with both parties equal. The Government had, however, been losing support in the country, mainly because of the Education Act and the Licensing Act. 'We were drowned in a torrent of gin and beer,' said Gladstone, who certainly, to judge by his pre-election comments, did not regard the trade union issue as of even minor electoral significance. The organised defection of labour supporters, in revolt against the Criminal Law Amendment Act, is, however, said to have contributed in some measure to the Government's defeat in the general election. The fact that the public houses were still the usual meeting-places for many trade unions no doubt helped to unite two hostile elements.

The Conservative Government in 1874 appointed another Commission, much to the trade unions' disgust. They feared that the whole question of trade union legislation would be re-opened, whereas all they wanted was the legalisation of picketing. Two working-class M.P.s had been returned in the election, with Liberal support, namely Alexander Macdonald, the miners' leader, and Thomas Burt, from the same industry, and both were offered places on the Commission. Burt refused; Macdonald accepted, but the hostility of the unions to the Commission forced him to resign from the chairmanship of their Parliamentary Committee. Hughes was a member, as was Russell Gurney, also known to be sympathetic to labour, and Roebuck. Nonetheless, the unions, with a few exceptions, boy-cotted the Commission, and the evidence from the side of labour came mainly from the Trades Councils of London and Glasgow.[16]

The Commission's Majority Report, signed by all except Macdonald, substantially confirmed the doubts about the need for any change in the Criminal Law Amendment Act. The Government, however, so far from taking advantage of this to avoid action, decided to ignore the Report, and introduced the Conspiracy and Protection of Property Bill.

This evoked surprisingly little opposition in or out of Parliament. The National Federation of Associated Employers, mainly in the textile industry, opposed it; it published a manifesto protesting against the growing power of the unions, which earned it a stern rebuke from *The Times*, as representing 'a movement tending politically to put asunder forces which have long been allied, and tending socially to draw capitalists and labour into two hostile camps'. But the attitude of employers generally was so complacent that *The Times* also re-marked on it.[17] The Bill, like the Employers and Workmen Bill of the same year, got a second reading without a division, and passed through the Lords with little criticism. The most likely explanation seems to be that Parliament, press and public were not greatly interested and somewhat bored with the whole subject.

The new Act delighted trade union leaders; one of them called it 'the greatest boon ever given to the sons of "toil".' It legalised peaceful picketing, the references to 'coercion' dis-appeared, and definitions of offences were tightened up. It removed for ever, as it seemed, the stigma of conspiracy from collective industrial action, for it accepted the minority view of the 1867 Commission, that an act committed by workers in concert, in furtherance of a trade dispute, should not rank as criminal conspiracy unless it were criminal when done by an individual. This was a doctrine viewed with considerable mis-givings by jurists and others with no special animus to trade unions, who thought the distinction should be preserved be-tween the responsibilities of an individual and those of a close-knit association of individuals in respect of wrongs committed by them.[18]

The freedom of action conferred by the Act was qualified in one important respect. It was recognised that the withdrawal of labour in an essential service could constitute not merely a hardship but a positive menace to the community, and two such services, which appeared at the time of paramount im-portance, were singled out for special treatment. The Act accordingly stipulated that a person employed by a municipal authority or other undertaking responsible for the supply of gas or water, who 'wilfully and maliciously' (that is, with deliberate intent or disregard for the consequences) broke his contract, 'knowing or having reasonable cause to believe that the probable consequences of his so doing, either alone or in com-bination with others, will be to deprive the inhabitants . . . wholly or to a great extent of their supply of gas or water', would be liable to prosecution. This, of course, did not conflict with the main principle that collective action by trade unions should not be specially culpable under the law, any more than did the proviso that breach of contract generally which was likely to endanger life or valuable property should also be an offence. The first provision was extended in 1919 to cover the supply of electricity.

The suggestion that trade unions should have the right to sue and be sued was again raised at this time, but the trade union movement was now well aware of its implications, and the idea was rejected by the T.U.C. in 1875.[19] The Act did not specifically confer immunity from court action on unions, but the fact that they were unincorporated might be held to produce the same effect. It was commonly assumed that, while the law recognised trade unions, they lacked any legal identity except that conferred by their registration with the Registrar of Friendly Societies. In 1876 there was passed the Trade Union (Amendment) Act. This included a definition of trade unions, which appeared innocuous enough at the time, but was later to assume great significance.

REFERENCES

1. W. S. Jevons: *op. cit.*, p. 31.
2. G. Howell: *op. cit.*, pp. 159–60.
3. W. H. G. Armytage: *op. cit.*, p. 35.
4. G. Howell: pp. 165–6, 169.
5. Eleventh and Final Report; A. E. Musson: *The Congress of 1868* (T.U.C., 1955).
6. Eleventh and Final Report, Appendix.
7. G. Howell: p. 168.
8. S. and B. Webb: *op. cit.*, pp. 274–6.
9. G. Howell: p. 178;
   S. and B. Webb: p. 269.
10. Sir F. Tillyard: *op. cit.*, p. 272.
11. H. Vester and A. H. Gardner: *Trade Unions and the Law* (Methuen, 1955), pp. 11–12.
12. G. Howell: p. 188.
13. *Ibid.*, pp. 192–207.
    A. G. Gardiner: *Life of Sir W. Harcourt* (Constable, 1923), I, pp. 254–7.
D

42 THE STATE AND THE TRADE UNIONS

14. Hedges and Winterbottom: *op. cit.*, pp. 112–13;
    H. Vester and A. H. Gardner: p. 14;
    British Working Class Movements — Select Documents, ed. G. D. H. Cole
    and A. W. Filson (Macmillan, 1951), pp. 574–7.
15. *British Working Class Movements*, p. 576;
    G. Howell: p. 236;
    cf. G. D. H. Cole and R. Postgate: *The Common People* (Methuen,
    1949), p. 397.
16. G. Howell: pp. 344, 348.
17. W. H. G. Armytage: pp. 134–6;
    G. Howell: p. 368.
18. S. and B. Webb: p. 291 n.;
    W. A. Orton: *The Economic Rôle of the State* (Hodge, 1950), p. 132.
19. G. Howell: pp. 385–6.

CHAPTER IV

THE NEW UNIONISM

THE expansion of the trade union movement did not wait on the repeal of the Criminal Law Amendment Act, often alleged to have so deleterious an effect on it. In the early 'seventies, the mood was one of optimism; the unions had been accorded a legal status, trade was booming, and the investigations resulting from the Sheffield Outrages and the case of Hornby v. Close had cleared the air, and restored a favourable climate of public opinion. The development of good relations between employers' and workers' organisations had been only interrupted by the troubles, and joint boards of conciliation and arbitration were spreading. The union leaders could relax. They practised the gospel of moderation they had preached to the Commission. They were content to accept capitalism and 'laissez-faire', and to regard themselves as partners of the employers. This outlook was most clearly reflected in the demand for a sliding-scale of wages related to the profitability of industry, instead of a minimum wage. So far as industrial legislation was thought desirable, they were content to leave it to the 'progressives' in Parliament, especially the Liberals, and the statutory industrial reforms of the 'seventies and 'eighties owed little to pressure from the T.U.C. or its Parliamentary Committee. It was left to the Radicals to proclaim that 'the path of legislation . . . must continue to be distinctly Socialistic'.[1]

The union leadership of the period has been criticised for this comparative inertia, but there was much to be said for a policy of studied moderation. The unions had fought for certain fundamental rights, and in the fight had pledged themselves not to abuse those rights. In Parliament there was much sympathy with labour aims, especially among the Radicals. Thus, a meeting to form an agricultural labourers' union might be chaired by an M.P.[2] This could hardly be construed as vote-catching, since agricultural labourers were not yet enfranchised, although of course it paid electorally to stand well with organised labour as a whole.

The so-called 'Great Depression' set in in 1875 and lasted, with occasional slackenings, for the next twenty years or so. Its repercussions, both economic and political, tended until lately to be much over-estimated. 'On the whole,' says a recent commentator, 'the workers did not suffer as a result of the so-called Great Depression, which, except in the later 'seventies, was a period of advance.' The reason was that, while the export trade experienced severe set-backs, industrial production increased, and prices declined sharply. Thus, although wages in general did not advance, the standard of living of those in stable employment improved. They could afford to buy more, and there were more things to buy. Labour was restless, and the period was marked by a rash of strikes, but many of them were not defensive, but in support of increased wages or reduced hours.[3]

This, of course, is to take an over-all view of the period and the subject. The onset of the recession and the recurrent crises of unemployment which marked it, had a dampening effect on labour spirits, and gave a serious set-back to the trade union movement, as it did to political socialism. As trade unionism recovered, it acquired a new bias. For a considerable proportion of the working population conditions were never anything but miserable. It was in this submerged mass that trade unionism found a new source of recruitment.

At this stage, and until the early years of the twentieth century, the great majority of trade unionists were artisans and factory workers in the establised trades, but now a new impulse and direction came from the organisation of 'general' unions of labourers. The first was Ben Tillett's Tea Workers and General Labourers' Union, closely followed by the Gasworkers and General Labourers' Union (later to become the National Union of General and Municipal Workers). Orthodox unionism, while by no means supine in regard to industrial action, preferred peaceful settlements, and no doubt its emphasis on friendly society functions reinforced this attitude. The new unions, on the other hand, represented workers with no traditions, little skills and no established rights to conserve; their *raison d'être* was to lay foundations rather than to build on existing ones. They were the people who, in Marx's phrase, believed they had nothing to lose but their chains: the lower grades whose employment was at best precarious, and who lived in, or on the verge of, destitution.

It followed that their unions were aggressive by nature, willing and eager to challenge the fundamentals of industry and of society itself. Their primary concern was with the improvement of their members' immediate conditions of employment, that is, pay and hours of work, and not with protection against unemployment, which was a natural concomitant of their callings, nor with sick benefits. They had no time for 'sliding scales' of wages, which implied acceptance of the profit system, while their earnings were so low that they had no room for a policy of give and take. Their rates of subscription must be very modest, and the first call on the funds was for strike pay. The old unions had disclaimed 'coercion', and had convinced themselves and many outside their ranks that trade unionism was quite consistent with individual liberty. They relied for their appeal on publicity and persuasion. The leaders of the new movement had no scruples about the use of coercion, whether for the employer or the 'blackleg'. 'In no period within my experience,' wrote Howell, 'was intimidation so openly proclaimed and condoned as it was in the early days of the New Unionism.'[4] It was not by chance that men of Irish extraction found the leadership of the labourers' unions a task after their own hearts.[5]

The new unionism, in its search for weapons against the capitalist order, found one to its hand in the new socialism. Both movements were united in their contempt for the old unionism, which they regarded as reactionary and a bastion of the existing social system. The Socialist Hyndman condemned it because, 'being also fundamentally unsectarian and un-political, they (its adherents) prevent any organised attempt being made by the workers as a class to form a definite party of their own'.[6] The dislike was mutual. Howell joined with Herbert Spencer in writing an introduction to the anti-socialist treatise, *A Plea for Liberty*. He and his kind saw in socialism a threat, not only to political understandings with the existing parties, which they believed were of good service to the labour cause, but to the very survival of trade unionism as an inde-pendent and purely industrial force. They were distrustful of State interference, and preferred as a rule to rely on industrial action.[7] In this they were representative of the great bulk of trade unionists and workers in general. Even Engels, writing in 1881, admitted that the working-class was 'the tail of the great Liberal Party'. The Labour Representation League, started in 1869, had made very little impact on labour, and less on the unions, largely because the existing system seemed to most of the leaders to be working quite well, to judge by the state of industry under 'laissez-faire'.[8]

Thus the combination of the new unionism and the new socialism proved of slow and uncertain growth. The former pro-duced great personalities like Ben Tillett, John Burns and Tom Mann, who were much influenced by the writings of Karl Marx and Henry George. They believed in the inevitability of the class struggle, and held that the State, not the trade unions, must accept a greater degree of responsibility for the welfare of the working-classes, including the care of the unemployed and indigent. At the same time, they were intensely practical, and placed the chief emphasis for the fulfilment of the immediate programme on industrial methods.

Trade union militancy paid dividends. The London match-girls' strike in 1888, and the dockers' strike in the following year, not only achieved their immediate ends, but focused public attention on, and evoked practical sympathy — £80,000 was subscribed by sympathisers in Britain and Australia to the dockers' strike funds — for those in the dark corners of the social scene, which were at the same time being lit up by investigators such as the shipowner, Charles Booth. In 1889 the Gas Workers' and General Labourers' Union compelled the employers to concede an eight-hour day. Bigger and better-organised unions were formed, like the United Textile and Factory Workers' Association (1887), the National Sailors' and Firemen's Union (1887), the Miners' Federation (1888), the Federation of Engineering and Shipbuilding Trades (1889) — which the Associated Society of Engineers refused to join — and other organisations of a more catholic kind, reminiscent in their titles and aims of the early nineteenth century, like the Labour Protection League and the National Labourers' Union. These developments had their natural reaction among employers, who tended to close their ranks in a resistance movement, as in the Shipping Federation (1890) and the Engineering Employers' Federation (1896).[9]

The T.U.C. was slow to succumb to the new influences in the labour world. It was not until 1890 that it finally endorsed the demand for a statutory eight-hour day, which had long been an issue of contention between its two wings. It refused, however, to identify itself with one political party; after all, the trade unionists of Durham and Northumberland were mainly Liberal, and those of Lancashire mainly Conservative.[10] In 1895 it expelled Keir Hardie and the rest of the purely political element from its councils. It continued to be merely a forum for debate, and refused to be the agency for the co-ordination of labour policy, whether industrial or political.

There were over a thousand strikes in 1889, and again in 1890. The rising temperature in industry prompted a good deal of discussion in high places about possible remedies. The Government in 1891 set up a Royal Commission, which, as usual, was denounced by some labour champions as a covert attack on trade unionism. The grounds for the charge were, to say the least, insubstantial. Of the Commission's membership, seven were trade union officials, including the redoubtable Tom

Mann; yet as recently as 1867 it had been thought gratifying by trade unions that they should even be invited to give evidence in their own cause.

Not for the first or last time in this connection, trade union fears proved groundless. The Majority Report was extremely non-committal; too non-committal for some of the members, like Tom Mann. It recognised dangers in the growth of trade unions and employers' associations, for instance the possibility of their combining together to 'repress individual energy and freedom of industrial experiment', or 'to control an industry injuriously to the public interest'. It found that employers still sometimes supported strikes 'as a mode of raising wages which the competition of employers generally and of surplus labour had brought down to a very low figure'. It declined, however, to recommend any change in the laws, and especially the introduction of any compulsion, on the grounds that disputes should be settled through effective voluntary machinery, relying on moral, not legal, sanctions. It discussed the desirability of 'a higher council of labour', a central body representative of all the parties concerned, and remote enough from the hurly-burly to make a dispassionate appraisal of industrial issues; but it decided against this because of the practical difficulties of constituting such a body. It did not go so far as Mann and Webb, who wanted a Ministry of Labour set up, but it agreed that a Government Department ought to be responsible for fostering the development of conciliation boards, which now covered only a comparatively small part of industry, and some of which were moribund. Three of the trade union representatives signed the Majority Report.

Perhaps the most significant feature of the Commission's work, in the light of later developments, was the conflict of opinion over the issue whether trade unions, having been legalised, should also be given 'a legal personality' and responsibility. Some of the Commission held that they should be allowed a degree of incorporation, which would entail liability to be sued in the courts for wrongful acts, including breach of collective agreements. This it was said, would be a 'most natural and reasonable solution', but, it was admitted, one for which perhaps public opinion was not yet ripe. The trade union representatives, on the other hand, held that 'to expose the large amalgamated societies of the country, with their accumulated funds, sometimes reaching a quarter of a million sterling, to be sued for damages by any employer .... or by any discontented member or non-unionist, for the action of some branch secretary or delegate, would be a great injustice'. They thought strikes a healthy reaction against existing social conditions, and urged that the State should end 'the present industrial anarchy' by substituting public for capitalist enterprise.[11]

The Commission as a whole took it for granted that, by the 'Labour Laws' (the legislation of the 'seventies) trade unions were exempt from civil action for damages, and that the question was whether this immunity ought to be modified. It was not long before this assumption was proved baseless, and the question of policy which had divided the Commission ceased to be an academic issue, and became one with profound political implications.

The State had already begun to take a more direct interest in labour relations. In 1886 Mundella, as President of the Board of Trade, had agreed that his Department should set up a Bureau of Labour Statistics. He went out of his way to disarm possible labour criticism by enlisting the services in this project of trade union officials, but it remained suspect, especially among employers. In 1893 it became a department of the Board. Its chief official was known as the Commissioner for Labour, and it published the *Labour Gazette*. The Conciliation Act of 1896 took matters a stage further, as the Commission had advocated, and made it the duty of the Board of Trade to foster conciliation processes in industry. It also empowered it to intervene to settle disputes by holding an inquiry where the public interest appeared to justify this, and by appointing a conciliator or board of conciliation at the request of either party, or an arbitrator on the application of both. It was an official recognition that the

State had an obligation to interfere, however delicately, in matters hitherto deemed the exclusive province of employers and workers.[12]

There was undoubtedly a recrudescence of anti-union feeling in the closing years of the nineteenth century, and the beginning of the twentieth. There were bitter disputes, partly stemming from the demand for trade union recognition —which many employers, including railway companies, refused to concede. The great engineering dispute in 1897 was seen by some as evidence of a deliberate campaign on the part of some powerful employers to smash trade unionism. It is doubtful if politics entered in, since socialism, whether supported by the unions or not, did not seem to the two political parties to menace their monopoly. 'All the Socialist-Radical bustle did not yet amount to very much in electoral terms.'[13] The Labour Representation League had been succeeded in 1882 by the Labour Electoral Association. In 1885 the number of working-class M.P.s rose to eleven, but all took the Liberal ticket. In 1892 Keir Hardie, John Burns and Havelock Wilson were returned as Labour M.P.s, along with twelve Lib-Labs, and in the next year the Independent Labour Party was set up by a conference of labour elements, including trade unions. But there were many trade unionists who stood aloof from this latest movement, including John Burns and Havelock Wilson. The T.U.C. still refused to sponsor a separate political party, and, as we have seen, in 1895 cast out the politicians, including Keir Hardie, and the traditionalists were firmly in the saddle. In the general election of 1895, not a single Labour candidate was successful. It was clear that the political labour movement had no hope of success unless it could induce the trade union movement to back it.[14]

Not until 1899 did the T.U.C. succumb to the pressure brought to bear on it in successive Conferences to espouse the political labour cause. In that year it authorised its Parliamentary Committee to call a conference of working-class organisations, and this conference agreed to support a separate Labour Group in Parliament. It rejected the Marxist approach on the one hand, and on the other the non-party approach of the old trade union school, and set up the Labour Representation Committee. (Its first Secretary, Ramsay MacDonald, had become a convert to the I.L.P. after being rejected as a parliamentary candidate by a local Liberal Association.) Still a great body of trade unionists, including the miners, refused to join. In the general election of 1900, only two out of fifteen candidates were returned — one of them, Richard Bell, went over to the Liberal Party in 1904 — and the number of Lib-Labs fell to eight.

Lack of money was a handicap. The Miners' Federation started a political fund in 1901, but it was not a party fund; indeed, the miners were among the last to desert the Liberal Party; although converted to the 'new unionism', they refused to embrace socialism or the idea of a Labour Party. The greatest handicap, however, was lack of enthusiasm. Industry was prosperous, wages were rising faster than prices, social legislation was making great strides, and all this in a state where 'laissez-faire' and capitalism still held sway.[15]

The fact was that the swing to the left, which had started in the 'eighties, had spent itself, and the socialists were beating the empty air. They had failed to make any real communion with the working-class or with organised labour. Even where the unions wanted parliamentary action, as the miners did in respect of the eight-hour day, they shied away from socialism. The new unionism had failed, after all, to take over the movement, and the official *Trade Unionist* could state in 1899: 'Thoughtful Trade Unionists have long entertained the conviction that strikes and lock-outs are barbarous methods of settling disputes. Besides its wastefulness, there is the factor of international competition. . . . Trade Union leaders see that British industry can only be held by the intelligent co-operation of all concerned.'[16]

There was much unrest, but it was essentially industrial. Even the craft unions were affected; the A.S.E., still the strongest of all the unions, was disturbed by the rapid growth

of machinery and the consequent dilution of labour. The
T.U.C., while shirking the task of giving a lead to labour, set
up another body, the General Federation of Trade Unions,
to be a central organisation with a national fund, which would
in particular deal with proposals for strikes and give financial
aid in approved cases. It received half-hearted support, for the
majority of the unions were determined not to relinquish to any
central body any part of their independence of action.

REFERENCES

1. S. and B. WEBB: *op. cit.*, pp. 337–8, 359–60, 368;
   cf. B. C. ROBERTS: *The Trades Union Congress 1868–1921* (Allen & Unwin,
   1958), pp. 360–1.
2. G. HOWELL: *op. cit.*, pp. 257–8.
3. H. PELLING: *Origins of the Labour Party, 1880–1900* (Macmillan, 1954),
   p. 8;
   G. HOWELL: p. 399.
4. G. HOWELL: p. 448.
5. *Labour's Turning Point (op. cit.)*, p. 30.
6. H. M. HYNDMAN: *Historical Basis of Socialism* (Kegan Paul, 1883), p. 288.
7. G. HOWELL: p. 450.
8. H. PELLING: p. 4.
9. J. H. RICHARDSON: *Industrial Relations in Great Britain* (I.L.O., 1933), p.
   79.
10. F. BEALEY and H. PELLING: *Labour and Politics, 1900–1906* (Macmillan,
    1958), pp. 18–19.
11. *Final Report of Royal Commission on Labour* (1894).
12. S. MACCOBY: *English Radicalism, 1886–1914* (Allen & Unwin, 1953), p.
    403;
    LORD AMULREE: *op. cit.*, p. 109.
13. S. MACCOBY: p. 191;
    A. G. GARDINER: *Life of George Cadbury* (Cassell, 1923), p. 27;
    H. PELLING: p. 8.
14. BEALEY and PELLING: pp. 181–3.
15. *Labour's Turning Point*, p. 76.
16. *Ibid.*, pp. 12–13;
    E. J. HOBSBAWM: 'General Labour Unions in Britain, 1889–1914' (*Economic History Review*, Vol. I, (1948–9), pp. 123–42).

CHAPTER V

THE EMANCIPATION OF THE TRADE UNIONS

THE Taff Vale judgment is often quoted as a flagrant example of the courts' hostility to trade unions. In fact, what it did was to make what could reasonably be regarded, and was indeed so regarded by people well qualified in such matters, as a perfectly logical interpretation of the law as it stood. That it also exposed a weakness or at least an ambiguity or uncertainty in the law, and that it had extremely awkward political implications, was no business of the courts.

In 1900, there was an unofficial strike of members of the Amalgamated Society of Railway Servants against the Taff Vale Railway Company in South Wales. Most railway companies, including this one, did not recognise the railway unions, and the Society reluctantly decided to support the strike by giving strike pay. The Company's management was uncompromising, rough methods were used to prevent the use of non-union labour and there was some damage to the Company's property. The Company brought civil actions against the Union, seeking an injunction to prevent interference with the Company's use of 'blackleg' labour and claiming damages in respect of actions of Union members. The case went to the House of Lords, which confirmed the verdict of a lower court against the Union, with damages assessed at £23,000.

The decision was not entirely unexpected, nor was it so completely odious to trade unionists in general as has often been maintained. The secretary of the Union concerned, Richard Bell, who had himself opposed the strike, considered that 'the privilege which for thirty years had been enjoyed by trade unions had been taken away from us . . . for abusing it'.[1] He thought the judgment would have a salutary chastening effect on trade unions, by reminding them that, if they did not exercise discipline, it would be imposed. The decision was apparently not taken by the trade unions as a deliberate attack on their movement, although this construction was quickly put on it by some of the socialist politicians, and was later taken up by writers on the period. The politicians' efforts to exploit it do not seem to have made any great impression on the rank and file trade unionists, and had little effect on their political beliefs.[2] Trade union leaders had, however, taken it for granted, as, it seems, had most people, that the Act of 1871 had safeguarded their organisations against attacks of this sort, especially as they remained unincorporated bodies, and that their liability was restricted to the criminal law, under the Conspiracy and Protection of Property Act. The decision, therefore, caused something of an uproar, and the Government in 1903 appointed a Royal Commission on Trade Disputes and Trade Combinations. It was boycotted by the unions, with the approval of the T.U.C., on various grounds: that a special inquiry was unnecessary; that the Commission had no trade union representatives; and that it was intended to pave the way for the introduction of compulsory arbitration.[3]

The Commission, which reported in 1906, was satisfied that the judgment did not raise any new issue of principle, and that it was quite consistent with the laws governing trade unions. It pointed out that the immunity from civil actions hitherto enjoyed by the unions had not derived from immunity conferred by statute, but from the impracticability of enforcing liability on a host of defendants — a difficulty applying not merely to trade unions, but to all unincorporated associations.

In 1883, a General Order, based on 'general considerations of equity quite irrespective of Trade Unions and Trade Union law', had decreed that in such cases one or more persons could sue or be sued as representative of the whole. Ten years later, in the case of Temperton v. Russell, the Court of Appeal held that this did not cover trade unions, but the judges in that case were not concerned with the question whether trade unions should or should not be liable to civil actions. The Royal Commission on Trade Disputes of 1891 had, however, assumed that trade unions were in fact immune. It had, in that light, considered the desirability of giving 'a legal personality' to unions, and had, in its Majority Report, suggested the possibility of incorporation to that end. In 1901 the Temperton *v*. Russell decision was over-ridden by the House of Lords (in the case of Duke of Bedford *v*. Ellis), when it was ruled that the General Order was of universal application. It should be noted that this last case was not at all concerned with trade unions. In the same year, the House of Lords, in the case of Quinn *v*. Leathem, confirmed that a combination of persons to injure another person was a breach of the civil law of conspiracy and liable to a claim in respect of the damage inflicted. Since a strike, to be successful, was bound to cause some hurt to the employer concerned, this judgment represented a serious threat to the trade unions.

In the Taff Vale case, the Report recalled, not only was it held by two of the judges in the House of Lords that a union could be sued by representative action, whether it was registered or not, but the unanimous conclusion was that it must have been Parliament's intention in 1871 that a trade union could be sued in its registered name. The Law Lords echoed the query of Mr. Justice Farrell in the lower court: 'If the contention of the defending Society were well founded, has the Legislature authorised the creation of numerous bodies of men capable of owning great wealth and of acting by agents, with absolutely no responsibility for the wrongs that they may do?' They concluded, as might have been expected, that of course Parliament could have had no such intention.

The Commission's Majority Report, signed by, among others, Sidney Webb, was most emphatic that the Taff Vale judgment was correct in its interpretation of the law as it stood, and furthermore, of the Legislature's intentions towards the trade unions as revealed in the existing statutes. 'No assurance of such immunity has ever been held out,' it affirmed; 'no public Commission as a body has represented that they ought to be exempt; no Government has promised that they would be exempt by forthcoming legislation; and no judge has pronounced that they are exempt.' It was equally emphatic that 'on the grounds of justice and equity . . . the objections against disturbing the law as laid down in the Taff Vale case appear insurmountable', since under the rule of law 'a wrong-doer should be made to redress his wrong' and, if trade unions were exempt, they would be uniquely privileged in that respect. The Commission saw 'no more reason that they should be beyond the reach of the law than any other individual, partnership, or institution'. It recommended that legislation should be passed (i) to declare trade unions legal associations; (ii) to make all strikes, including sympathetic strikes, legal except those involving crime or breach of contract; (iii) to protect trade unions against prosecution for unauthorised actions of branch agents; (iv) to separate trade unions' benefit funds and give them immunity; (v) to permit unions to acquire corporate status; (vi) to ensure that combinations should be immune from legal action except in cases of criminal conspiracy; and (vii) to revise the law as regards picketing, in order to prevent violence.[4]

Sidney Webb added his own Memorandum, remarkable for its detachment, in which he challenged certain of the assumptions which employers and unions, as well as Government, had long taken for granted as fundamental to the whole system of industrial relations. He denied that strikes between unions and employers were a natural and proper ingredient of industry, and affirmed that society had too much of a stake in the good conduct of industry to allow and even connive at a sort of damaging civil warfare. He wrote: 'I cannot accept the assumption underlying the Report that a system of organised struggles between employers and workmen, leading inevitably now and again to strikes and lock-outs . . . represents the only method, or even a desirable method, by which to settle the conditions of employment. A strike or a lock-out . . . necessarily involves so

THE EMANCIPATION OF THE TRADE UNIONS 57

much dislocation of industry; so much individual suffering; so much injury to third parties, and so much national loss, that it cannot, in my opinion, be accepted as the normal way of settling an intractable dispute. Moreover, from the point of view of the community, such a method has the drawback that it affords no security . . . that the resultant conditions of employment will be such as not to be gravely injurious to the community as a whole' (for example, by 'sweating' or restriction of output). 'I cannot believe that a civilised community will permanently continue to abandon the adjustment of industrial disputes . . . and incidentally the regulation of the conditions of life of the mass of its people . . . to what is, in reality, the arbitrament of private war.' He recommended, therefore, a system of conciliation and arbitration on the lines of those already operating in Australia and New Zealand.[5]

The Taff Vale decision had aroused the trade union movement from its torpor, and, while the leaders still remained cool to political activity in general, they recognised that all the political forces available must be mobilised for remedial legislation on this particular matter. The Labour Representation Committee was one obvious agency. One of its greatest frustrations hitherto had been that either the aims it could avow as peculiarly its own were looked at somewhat askance by the trade unions as industrial objectives which might be achieved by industrial means, and were therefore not the business of Parliament, or they were of the kind which, to judge by experience, could be considered well within the scope of the existing political parties. It could no longer be argued that only a workers' party would promote social reform. Throughout the nineteenth century, the State had gradually been accepting an ever greater measure of responsibility for those workers who were regarded as unable to protect themselves, namely children and women. In this process, outstanding champions of their cause were drawn from the ranks of both Whigs and Tories, including employers. John Fielden, a great mill-owner, and Richard Wood, another employer, were conspicuous, as were

E

Tories like Richard Oastler and Michael Sadler, and of course Lord Ashley, later Earl of Shaftesbury, to name but a few. As investigations, both official and unofficial, revealed the evils of the industrial system, and public opinion became more enlightened, the movement gained impetus. The development of a government inspectorate was a potent factor. It was obvious at the turn of the century that the State had abandoned 'laissez-faire' for ever so far as labour was concerned, and that the extension of paternal government to cover the sick, aged and unemployed would find powerful and increasing support in both political parties. The widening of the franchise was bound to exert an additional incentive.

Here, nevertheless, was an issue ready-made for M.P.s with a direct loyalty to the trade union movement. There was every reason at this moment to have representatives of organised labour in Parliament, not to displace the Liberal Party, but to act as a 'pressure group'. Organised labour rallied to the cause. In 1902–3 the membership of the unions affiliated to the Labour Representation Committee rose from 469,000 to 861,000; by 1906–7, it was close to one million. In 1903 the T.U.C. passed a resolution pledging the unions to support it.[6]

The main hope of reform, however, was in the Liberal Party; and, as most trade unionists still looked to this Party as their natural champion, so did Liberals regard it as their natural duty to promote labour's cause. Many of them, including their leader Campbell-Bannerman, favoured direct labour representation. 'We want a hundred working men in Parliament,' said George Cadbury, a confirmed Liberal, and, with others, he fostered privately and in the press an electoral alliance between Liberals and Labour. In 1903, the political labour movement was officially committed to independence, but this was little more than a brave gesture. The Liberals, on the other hand, were justifiably confident that the popular revulsion from the Conservatives' nostrum of Tariff Reform (and higher prices) would alone assure them of success in the next General Election. Even so, meetings between the two were arranged and, although formal negotiations were barred, an unofficial understanding was arrived at. In a good many constituencies, (about thirty altogether), the Liberals left the field clear to the Labour candidates.[7]

The Liberal Party's victory in the election owed little or nothing to the Taff Vale issue, and the electoral arrangement with the L.R.C. mainly benefited the latter's candidates.[8] Twenty-nine of them were returned, as well as fourteen miners' M.P.s and a number of Lib-Labs. There was little to choose between these groups, or between them and the Liberals. They saw no inconsistency between their representation of working-class constituents, and sympathy with Liberal Party doctrine. If they had, their trade union allies, who kept a vigilant eye on them, would have soon called them to order. The return of a substantial bloc of labour spokesmen was nevertheless bound to impress both the other parties. In any case, Liberal lawyers and Liberal candidates had freely inveighed against the Taff Vale decision, and when elected were not slow to redeem their pledges. Some of them, like Asquith, had been consulted by the Parliamentary Committee as to the line of action to be pursued in order to restore the trade union position. There were Liberal M.P.s, such as Lloyd George, who was a member of the new Government, who were of fairly humble origins, and highly sympathetic to working-class aspirations. There was, therefore, no question but that remedial legislation would be introduced. A bill was promptly introduced on the lines of the Royal Commission's findings.

The Cabinet, while agreed that legislation was necessary, was divided on the issue of the degree of immunity to be given to trade union funds. This was hardly surprising, since the same was true even of the trade unions' leaders and representatives. Some of them did not want the Bill, or only partial immunity from legal action. Richard Bell (who in 1902 became Chairman of the Labour Representation Committee) thought it reasonable that trade unions should be treated in the same way as corporations, especially as this would mean that their agreements would be legally enforceable. The Government lawyers, including Asquith, wanted to rely on restriction of the law of agency in its application to unions. The Prime Minister, Campbell-Bannerman, on the other hand, was a Radical, and, fearing, as he put it, that the courts would 'run a coach and six' through any such fine distinctions, demanded a more positive and sweeping enactment.[9] Ultimately, the Cabinet decided on the former approach. The Labour group introduced their own Bill, as drafted on behalf of the T.U.C. Parliamentary Committee. This went much farther than the same body's earlier proposals, for delay and frustration had only discredited the moderates. The Bill went all the way in demanding complete legal immunity. To the shocked surprise of his Cabinet colleagues, who had not been warned or consulted, the Prime Minister announced acceptance of it in principle. Even Labour was taken aback. Philip Snowden thought his action was 'unprecedented', and others dubbed it 'Machiavellian'.

Asquith's cautious attitude was shared by many others. He believed the Taff Vale and Quinn v. Leathem judgments were sound in law, while regretting that 'the long practical immunity' of the unions had been distorted thereby. He strongly objected, however, to the 'putting words into a statute which gave one class, labour, a privilege not enjoyed by other classes'. He very reluctantly gave way to the Prime Minister, on condition that the same immunity should be given to employers. Curiously enough, this latter proviso was apparently the part most disliked by Balfour, leader of the Opposition, who thought combinations of employers could be at least as dangerous as those of workers. But his party was concerned at this juncture only with regaining some of its lost popularity, and was resolved to do nothing which could be construed as anti-labour, and might thereby weaken its already precarious position. This helps to explain why the Bill, which aroused so much genuine apprehension, went through both Houses without any difficulty. Of the Bill, Lord Lansdowne, the Opposition leader in the Lords, said privately: 'I regard it as conferring excessive

privileges upon the trade unions, as conferring excessive privileges upon one class and on one class only — privileges in excess
of what the most trusted exponents of their views have formerly
asked for, privileges fraught with danger to the community, and
likely to embitter the industrial life of this country; but I also
hold that it is useless for us, situated as we are, to oppose this
measure.'[10]

The first three sections of the Trade Disputes Act were far-
reaching, but would probably have aroused comparatively
little excitement, since they were designed to complete the
process of putting orthodox trade union activities in trade disputes beyond the reach of the law. A concerted act in such cases
was not to be actionable unless it were so if done by an individual; in other words, the decision in Quinn v. Leathem was
thrown overboard, and the latitude already given in respect of
criminal cases was now extended to civil cases. Peaceful picketing was legalised, without qualification. An act was to be no
longer illegal because it induced breach of contract or interfered with another's business or freedom to dispose at will of his
labour; thus a hallowed doctrine was quietly finished off and
buried. Section 4 went very much further; it decreed that 'an
action against a trade union, whether of workmen or masters,
or against any members or officials thereof on behalf of themselves and all other members of the trade union in respect of
any tortious act alleged to have been committed by or on behalf
of the trade union, shall not be entertained by any Court.'

The Act in effect rejected the views of the courts and of
Royal Commissions that trade unions, like other bodies, should
be answerable to the law for wrongs committed on their behalf.
Professor Dicey considered that it conferred upon a trade union
'a freedom from civil liability for the commission of even the
most heinous wrong by the union or its servants, and in short
confers upon every trade union a privilege and protection not
possessed by any other person or body of persons, whether corporate or incorporate, throughout the United Kingdom. . . . It
makes a trade union a privileged body exempted from the

ordinary law of the land. No such privileged body has ever before been deliberately created by an English Parliament.' [11]

Criticism on these lines was frequent, especially in legal quarters, where the implications of the statute, and its break with traditional canons of justice, were appreciated to the full. The process of emancipating the trade unions was surely complete; to many it seemed to have gone too far in the removal of standard restraints and safeguards. Immunity from civil action was not even, on the face of things, confined to wrongs committed by a union in connection with a trade dispute, while, where a trade dispute was concerned, the immunity conferred was not confined to members of trade unions. Even friends of the labour movement were apprehensive; the extraordinary license conferred could so easily be exploited and abused by leaders conscious of their new power. [12]

The Act was in one way the logical culmination of nineteenth century trade union legislation. Indeed, some observers found its roots in a reaction against the early repression of labour organisation. [13] Yet in a sense it was quite contrary to the tendencies of the time. The State had of late been progressively renouncing the doctrine of 'laissez-faire', and had been increasingly acting on the assumption that it must accept responsibility for the social welfare of the community. To this end, individuals and sectional interests must be regulated. Collectivism was replacing individualism. By the Act, too, the rights of the individual were in a measure made subject to the collective will; but the agents for this were, not the State, but self-created corporations, designed to serve their own particular sectional ends, and given the widest freedom in their choice of methods, including coercion.

This kind of legislation obviously owed nothing directly to socialism. Socialism in some degree was being preached by all parties; but this Act was in conflict with basic socialist tenets, by which the State was to be the arbiter in fundamental matters of common concern. The Act enhanced the prestige of the Labour Party, but only because the Party was specially identified with the trade union movement. It was not a vindication of socialism, for neither the Party nor the movement was socialist. If the Party's views carried weight in Parliament, it was not because it had any great electoral significance as yet, but because it was regarded as the embodiment of a specialist knowledge of labour issues and labour aspirations. This knowledge was lacking among most other M.P.s. They had recognised in the Trade Disputes Act that there was a trade union problem, but to them it was essentially a constitutional one. They were not, and in the circumstances could not have been, well-informed on trade unions as such.

As in the case of the earlier trade union Acts, the desire of Parliament was to be rid of the problem in the easiest way. Lawyers had made it; let the lawyers devise the remedy. The most plausible explanation of Parliament's haste in passing the Act was the desire to put an end once and for all to vexing legal quibbles and resulting political controversies about the status and functions of trade unions. This, it seemed, had now been done beyond dispute, and it was generally assumed, by all concerned, that henceforth the unions' freedom of operation would be untrammelled. It was not long, however, before the unions were again challenged in the courts.

This time the challenge was in regard to their political activities. For forty years unions had been subsidising candidates for public office, and giving them financial support when elected. They were not as a rule committed to any one party, and at this stage the powerful miners' union had its own group of M.P.s quite separate from the Labour Party. The fact remained that the Labour Party was largely dependent for its electoral funds, and for the maintenance of its M.P.s — since M.P.s still had no official salaries — on trade union contributions. The Registrar accepted political activity as a legitimate function of trade unions, and as late as 1907 a High Court decision (Steele v. South Wales Miners' Federation) had confirmed this attitude.[14]

In 1908 a branch of the Amalgamated Society of Railway

Servants, through its secretary, Osborne, sought an injunction against the Union to restrain it from spending its funds on political objects. The court rejected the claim, but it was successful in the Court of Appeal, and this decision was upheld unanimously by the judges in the House of Lords (1909). Trade Unions, it was held, although not incorporated, were, like corporations, governed in regard to their status and privileges by Acts of Parliament, and the Acts similarly recited and restricted the purposes in regard to which they enjoyed their statutory privileges. The 1876 Trade Union (Amendment) Act defined a trade union as a combination 'for regulating the relations between workmen and masters, or between workmen and workmen, or between masters and masters, or for imposing restrictive measures on the conduct of any trade or business'. There was no mention of political activity, *ergo* political activity was 'ultra vires', and the application of union funds to it illegal. It appeared, too, that there was an issue of public policy involved, for this particular Union insisted that the candidates it sponsored must accept 'the conditions of the Labour Party', which meant, among other things, that all members of the Union were compelled to subscribe to one party, regardless of their own political sympathies.[15]

The urgent need to remedy the position established by the judgment once again gave a common objective to the trade union movement and the Labour Party. The Union involved in the judgment wreaked a bitter vengeance on the branch that had instigated the action; it was forthwith closed, and Osborne expelled from the Union with the loss of eighteen years' subscriptions.[16] But the situation required more than useless reprisals.

Not only were unions debarred from political activity, which meant a serious curtailment of their liberties, whatever their political sympathies might be; according to the Osborne ruling, they were going beyond their legal province in discharging a most important and traditional function, the provision of benefits for their members, since this too was not explicitly stipulated in the defining statutes. As in the Taff Vale case, the judgment was not entirely distasteful to the whole trade union movement; 'there was a section of the membership which greeted the Osborne decision with satisfaction, because it wanted the trade unions to cease supporting the Labour Party'.[17] But most union leaders disliked the restriction in principle and in practice. For the Labour Party, the situation was even more critical, since it threatened the Party's very existence. Sixteen M.P.s had to be deprived of their salaries. Trade union appeals to members for voluntary subscriptions for political purposes evoked a disappointing response; the powerful Amalgamated Society of Engineers, with over 107,000 members, could find only about 5000 to offer a contribution of one shilling each.[18] Yet the legal impediments did not appear to exert a very damaging effect on the electoral fortunes of the Party, although they may possibly have retarded its further progress. In 1906, twenty-nine Labour M.P.s had been returned, with fourteen miners' M.P.s, as well as some Lib-Labs. In 1909 the Miners' Federation's M.P.s joined the Party. In the first 1910 general election, the total of Labour M.P.s was forty, and, in the second election of that year, it rose slightly to forty-two. The operation of the two-party system, of course, also militated against the rise of a third party. The Liberal Party had again supported Labour, except in Scotland.

It is sometimes alleged that the Government was reluctant, for party reasons, to remove the curb on trade unions' political work, and that it delayed amending legislation as long as possible. This is hardly compatible with the support given by the Liberal Party to Labour candidates. In fact, the Government was preoccupied with other and, to it, more grave matters at the outset of its existence. Its majority was precarious, and while it could justifiably depend on Labour support in Parliament, the large Irish group (twice the Labour strength) made Home Rule the crucial voting factor. The Parliament Act and the National Insurance Act of 1911 would alone have been onerous enough tasks for the first year, but the principle of payment of M.P.s (£400 a year) was also established, in direct response to the Osborne judgment. The Prime Minister, Asquith, was quite categorical in his opinion of the Osborne judgment; he told the House of Commons that 'the limitations which the Osborne judgment put upon trade unions was not a politic one, nor one that was contemplated at the time of the legislation by which the present status of the Trade Unions was conferred upon them'. As with the Taff Vale judgment, however, he refused to believe that the answer was to have no restraints whatsoever, as not only Labour M.P.s but Radicals contended. He insisted that it would be wrong to compel all members of trade unions to subscribe financially to one party which as citizens they might not favour. This time his views prevailed, and the result was the Trade Union Act of 1913.[19]

The Act amplified the definition of trade unions to include the provision of benefits to members as a statutory object. A union could, however, have objects in addition to their statutory objects, provided these were authorised by their rules. They were thus given latitude to extend their functions as circumstances might require. They were specifically permitted to pursue political objects, provided the consent of the majority of their memberships were first secured by ballot vote. The political funds were to be kept separate from the rest, and members not wishing to contribute to these funds could 'contract-out' of the obligation to do so, by claiming exemption, without loss of union rights. The Parliamentary Committee of the T.U.C. and the Labour Party were fairly content with the Act, the more so as there had been ominous moves from employers and Conservatives to take advantage of the situation to re-impose restrictions on trade unions.[20]

REFERENCES

1. BEALEY and PELLING: op. cit., pp. 74–5.
2. Ibid., pp. 75–6, 87–8.
3. Report of Royal Commission on Trade Disputes (1906), p. 2;
   LORD ASKWITH: Industrial Problems and Disputes (Murray, 1920), p. 94;
   S. and B. WEBB: op. cit., pp. 604–5.

4. *Report of Royal Commission*, pp. 3–17;
   HEDGES and WINTERBOTTOM: *op. cit.*, pp. 135–6, 140–1.
5. *Report of Royal Commission*, p. 18.
6. S. and B. WEBB: p. 604.
7. A. G. GARDINER: *Life of George Cadbury* (*op. cit.*), pp. 81–3;
   BEALEY and PELLING: pp. 157–8.
8. BEALEY and PELLING, pp. 258, 265, 288.
9. J. A. SPENDER: *Life of Campbell-Bannerman* (Hodder & Stoughton, 1923),
   II, pp. 277–80.
10. BEALEY and PELLING: p. 81;
    J. A. SPENDER and C. ASQUITH: *Life of Lord Oxford and Asquith* (Hutchinson, 1932), I, pp. 182–4, II, p. 280;
    VISCOUNT SNOWDEN: *An Autobiography* (Ivor Nicholson & Watson, 1934),
    I, p. 144;
    E. HUGHES: *Keir Hardie* (Allen & Unwin, 1956), p. 132;
    R. JENKINS: *Mr. Balfour's Poodle* (Heinemann, 1954), pp. 26–7;
    B. E. DUGDALE: *A. J. Balfour* (Hutchinson, 1936), II, pp. 38–9.
11. A. V. DICEY: *op. cit.*, Introdn., pp. xlv–xlvi.
12. S. and B. WEBB: p. 606.
13. A. V. DICEY: Introdn., p. xlviii.
14. HEDGES and WINTERBOTTOM: p. 102.
15. *Ibid.*, pp. 102–3.
16. R. C. K. ENSOR: *England, 1870–1914* (Oxford, Clarendon Press, 1952),
    p. 438 n.
17. B. C. ROBERTS: *The Trades Union Congress* (*op. cit.*), p. 225.
18. R. C. K. ENSOR: p. 438.
19. SPENDER and ASQUITH: *op. cit.*, I, pp. 365–6.
20. B. C. ROBERTS: p. 257

CHAPTER VI

DOCTRINES AND DISCONTENTS

THE Labour Party remained little more than a 'pressure group', working in association with and subservient to the Liberal Party, a state of affairs towards which the divergencies between it and the T.U.C. and the General Federation of Trade Unions contributed. Its internal stresses were signalised by the replacement, as its leader, of Keir Hardie, who was suspect in certain trade union quarters, by Ramsay Mac-Donald, and by the appearance in 1911 of the rival British Socialist Party, which was the Social Democratic Federation in another guise. Like the S.D.F., it seemed to have little prospect of weaning labour from its moderate political policies, especially now that the unions had nothing more to win in the way of legal recognition. As late as 1913, it was openly acknowledged in the T.U.C. that there were comparatively few socialists in the ranks of the unions, and that the workers' attitude to Labour policies at by-elections was lukewarm.[1]

Mention has been made of the National Insurance Act. Some Socialists and trade unionists were inclined to look a little coldly at the Bill, though for different reasons: the former because they thought the State should bear the whole cost of such social benefits, the latter because the insurance scheme would presumably detract from the appeal of trade unions, much of whose work was in this field. The Government, however, won over most trade union representatives by including unions among the 'approved societies' which would help administer sick and unemployment arrangements. Thus the unions found themselves given a new and pleasing status, as agents of the Government in welfare matters, with their attraction to workers thereby enhanced rather than diminished.

As far back as 1891 the House of Commons had adopted a Fair Wages Resolution whose object was to ensure that the wages paid by Government contractors should be at 'standard' rates. In 1909 a new Resolution was passed which laid it down that contractors must observe rates of pay and hours of work 'not less favourable than those commonly recognised by employers and trade societies', or, in the absence of such standards, those operated by 'good employers'. The Government went out of its way to make it clear that it had no intention to enter the field of wage determination; on the contrary it was by the Resolution binding itself to 'accept as Fair Wages those rates of wages which prevail in any particular trade; the rate that has been fixed by negotiation between employers and workmen'. The principle of the Resolution was recommended to and generally accepted by Local Authorities. (In 1946 the Resolution was strengthened, by agreement with the T.U.C. and the British Employers' Confederation, so as to cover conditions of work, to secure the observance of collective agreements and arbitrations, and to guarantee freedom to workers to belong to trade unions.)

There was one item in the great social legislation of the period which, in the context of this survey, has a special significance. It was all very well for the State to encourage the development of trade unions of workers and employers and leave to them the settlement of wages and conditions within their territories; but there was a section of industry where this rule did not apply. The investigations of Charles Booth, Seebohm Rowntree and others had shocked public opinion by their revelations of the appalling situation of workers in the 'sweated industries', where organisation did not exist, and Sir Charles Dilke and others had been campaigning for years for legislation to protect them. The Liberal *Daily News* in 1906 organised a Sweated Industries Exhibition. In 1909 the Government acknowledged an obligation in this direction, when Winston Churchill, as Home Secretary, introduced the Trade Boards Bill. The Act of 1909 authorised the Board of Trade to set up a board, consisting of workers' and employers' representatives and independent members, to fix a legal minimum wage in any trade in which the wages were 'exceptionally low as compared with those paid in other employments', and four such trades were immediately specified, namely, tailoring, chain-making, machine-made lace and net finishing and paper-box making. The system was subsequently extended to cover other trades. For the first time since the Tudor and Stuart legislation had gone, the State accepted a measure of direct responsibility for wage-fixing. In the previous year an Act had prescribed an eight-hour day for coal-miners.[2]

In spite of such benefits, the years immediately preceding the First War were marked by a great deal of unease both in politics and in industry. The Liberals had achieved a vast amount, in the face of unscrupulous opposition, and had apparently exhausted themselves in the process. They were perpetually harassed by the Irish Question, and the international situation was threatening. The economic situation was deteriorating. In the Great Depression, prices had fallen, and wages had, if anything, advanced, but the end of the century saw a change. Money wages in general continued to rise, but they were now being outstripped by prices, which between 1906 and 1914 rose by about sixteen per cent.[3] British industry was feeling the draught of foreign tariffs and competition, while production was falling away, a development in which trade union restrictive practices played a not insignificant part.[4] The skilled workers fared better than the unskilled, which helped to explain the comparative quiescence of union leadership, since their organisations still predominantly represented the skilled workers. Conversely, it accounted for the growing dissatisfaction of the more vulnerable workers, including miners, whose wages were tied to a sliding-scale of coal prices, with orthodox labour policies, both industrial and political.

Economic discontents were reinforced by others. There was a feeling of frustration in the labour ranks. The State had given the fullest recognition to trade unions, but the long struggle with employers on the same issue was not yet resolved, for instance in the railway industry, where it looked as if a trial of strength would be necessary. There was impatience, too, with political parties. The Labour Party had made comparatively little impact, and it was suspected that vested interests were too strongly entrenched for the working-class to make any real impression on them. The Osborne case judgment was quoted as proof of class-prejudice and, with more justice, the flagrantly obstructive tactics of the House of Lords.

Once again, therefore, there was a swing away from orthodox political action, and a reversion to the old panacea of direct industrial action to compel a fundamental reform of society. The reform was to establish workers' control. This time there were more systematised forces behind the movement. The doctrine of 'direct action' derived partly from French syndical-ism, seeking the disintegration of the capitalist structure and its replacement by a workers' society, through repeated local or sectional strikes, culminating in a triumphant general strike which would leave the trade unions in control of their respective industries. Partly it owed its inspiration to 'industrial union-ism', as expounded by the American Industrial Workers of the World. Industrial Unionism meant that all workers in an in-dustry would be embraced in a mass union, instead of being organised on a 'horizontal' basis, as in the case of the craft unions. It had as its gospel the view that employers' and workers' interests were utterly irreconcilable, and that the way to crack the shell of society was to build up within it a structure of industrial unions which would disrupt the social fabric. Here, too, the method of exerting pressure would be the 'total' strike, including the collective or general strike, using any methods expediency might dictate.[5]

These doctrines had an affinity with Marxism, as preached by the Socialist Labour Party, established in 1903, which also was based on class-war, serving the ends, however, of a political movement.

All those revolutionary factions were agreed that the trade

unions must play a decisive part in the overthrow of society as then constituted. They were also agreed that, as things were, the unions were bastions of the capitalist system. The unions must, therefore, they said, be re-cast in a new form, divesting themselves of such distracting and enervating functions as the provision of benefits. In particular they must be fused into a few single, comprehensive organisations, thus eliminating the over-lapping and fragmentation which now characterised the move-ment, and facilitating a much closer degree of common effort. Their leadership must become dynamic and militant. In short, there must be war *à l'outrance* not only against the State but, as an essential preliminary, against the old-fashioned unions and their old-fashioned leaders, as well as against the allegedly supine Labour Party.

It was not only extremists who saw the need for greater harmony and cohesion in the trade union movement. Trade unions had grown up almost haphazard and had proliferated without a plan, and there might be a score of them elbowing and snarling at each other in the same industry. This sprawling mass was growing, not spectacularly — except in spasms, as in the 'nineties — but steadily: by 1906 it had topped the two million mark, and after 1910 the pace quickened until by 1914 this total had almost doubled. But there was not, and in the circumstances could not be, any central direction or common aim. In 1910 there were around 1200 unions representing $2\frac{1}{2}$ million members, many of them very small and local. The T.U.C. plodded along in the wake of the movement, claiming loyalty but not enthusiasm from perhaps three-fifths of the aggregate of unionists. It was little more than a sounding-board, and not a very effective one. The General Federation of Trade Unions, formed in 1899, remained very much a minority organisation. Clearly trade unionism was due for another phase of re-invigoration and re-orientation, if it were to keep pace with labour aspirations.[6]

In the nature of things it was inevitable that the new impulse should be in one particular direction. That the unions should pause and re-group their forces was eminently natural and desirable, and did not of itself presage any alteration in course. The movement was spreading to include the black-coated workers, but these were not likely to inspire any marked deviation from the orthodox. The energy that could transform the movement was clearly latent in the great body of unskilled labourers. Angry new eddies had arisen from this submerged mass in the 'nineties. They had swirled fretfully around the pillars of the old unionism, but these had stood firm. The new unionism, so far as the lower-paid ranks were concerned, had dissipated itself in a multitude of sketchy organisations. This time the forces must be united and harnessed to a common cause.

Tom Mann had been a leader of the 'new' unionism in the 'nineties. In 1910 he returned from Australia with his own amalgam of industrial unionism and syndicalism. His programme was to foster strikes in preparation for 'the General Strike of national proportions' which would force capitalism to abdicate the control of industry in favour of workers' organisations. He appreciated that transport, including sea transport, was the key industry for this purpose, and he set himself to link together the existing associations of dockers, seamen and transport workers other than railway-men. With the aid of Ben Tillett, another stalwart survivor of the 'new' unionism, he created in 1910 the National Transport Workers' Federation, which, they thought, could in time be welded into one union. In fact, it hardly justified the title of federation, nor was it national, but it was symbolic of the aims being declared by syndicalists in every major industry.

The new militancy began to gain expression before trade union organisation in the industries concerned could be geared to it. Indeed, in many cases it was almost independent of the unions; strikes frequently were unofficial or were only reluctantly fathered by the official leadership. The most notable of the series that started in 1910 and continued for the next four years, were in mining — where bitterness and mistrust were

F

endemic, and where, therefore, the new ideas found a receptive soil — and in transport. They were marked by an indiscipline and sometimes a savagery reminiscent of an earlier time, for they were in one sense a struggle against authority. Economic motives were of course present; these were intensified by the fact that wages were now lagging behind prices. The issue of trade union recognition entered in, as on the railways and in the shipping industry, where the unions were either not recognised at all by employers, or at best were highly suspect. In some instances, however, the strikes were directed almost as much against the established union leadership as against the employers. The painfully wrought, and often inadequate, machinery of negotiation, where it existed, was regarded with contempt by the extremists as the adjunct of an outworn system, and as an acknowledgment of a common purpose as between employers and labour which did not and could not exist. How could the two parties bargain together if there were no identity of interest? Tom Mann therefore advocated the abandonment of collective agreements. It was a simple doctrine, and one that appealed to the constituents of such as Mann, reared in a rough school, where brute strength was a condition of survival.[7]

There were dangers and weaknesses implicit in this movement. Tom Mann, Ben Tillett and others of their kind were forceful personalities, but the material with which they worked was explosive and unpredictable, lacking the coherence and tradition of a craft. Its handling would demand more than appeal to passion, for a spark was liable to set off a chain-reaction of large-scale dimensions, beyond the control of any central agency. Many of the leaders were not syndicalists, but they believed, with Bismarck, that war would breed solidarity, and that organisation could follow as a second stage.

In 1910 there were unofficial strikes in the north-east of England, in the coal-mines and on the railways. A strike in the Lancashire cotton industry, with the slightest of justifications, reached such proportions that the Board of Trade had to intervene. There was a great stoppage in the shipbuilding industry, starting with a local repudiation by the men of an agreement made by the Boilermakers' Society. Towards the end of the same year, there was a vicious unofficial miners' strike in South Wales, where Tom Mann had been active and had found many converts, marked by mob rioting. The police, unable to control the situation, asked for help, which was sent in the form of a body of Metropolitan police and troops. Winston Churchill, as Home Secretary, was assailed on the one hand for this resort to force, and on the other for not taking measures more promptly. It is interesting, therefore, to observe the verdict of an eminent modern historian on the episode: 'His (Churchill's) delay, though it sacrificed property, almost certainly saved life; but it may be that more drastic action would have checked the rise of strike-violence in the two following years.' [8]

This is likely, for the extremists were closely watching the reaction of the Government to thrusts which would probe the resolution of the State as well as that of the employers. Would the State, as the embodiment of capitalism, crush the campaign against employers, or could it be coerced to the point of insisting on the workers' demands being conceded in full? That a powerful section of the union leadership was prepared to use any and every weapon to force the hand of the Government there was no doubt. This reckless attitude was distrusted by the T.U.C., and denounced at the time by orthodox champions of the labour movement, such as Arthur Henderson, J. H. Thomas and Keir Hardie. Arthur Henderson and George Barnes, both Labour M.P.s, introduced a Bill to make strikes illegal unless thirty days' advance notice were given. The Government was in a vulnerable position, for the possible disruption of the economy at a time of international crisis was a frightening prospect. It was well aware that revolutionary elements played a part in the current industrial unrest.[9]

In 1911, an astonishingly successful seamen's strike, in which a body of men for whom concerted action was peculiarly difficult defeated the strongest of all employers' associations, the Shipping Federation, set off a series of strikes in the dock areas.

These were essentially local in character, although the Transport Workers' Federation sought to give them a national complexion. Troops had to be used to quell rioting, and in Liverpool two men were shot. An official railway strike, on a national scale, then threatened to paralyse the transport system of the country. The Prime Minister offered a Royal Commission to investigate the railway unions' grievances, but this was rejected, and the strike began. There was further rioting, with loss of life. Lloyd George, President of the Board of Trade, who had averted a national railway strike in 1907, was authorised by the Government to procure a settlement, and succeeded in doing so, with the backing of the Labour Party.

Early in 1912, the Miners' Federation called a strike of its million-strong membership, in support of the claim for a minimum wage. Government attempts at mediation broke down against the intransigence of both employers and Federation, but the Government nevertheless insisted on passing the Minimum Wage Bill, which, while it conceded the principle of minimum wages, which in fact the Government had offered before the strike, rejected the demand for the national determination of actual rates, which had precipitated the strike. Thus, the strike gained the miners nothing. For the Federation, it had been more than an all-out effort to secure better conditions for its membership. The Federation had been fighting to establish the principle of national, as distinct from local or district, settlements. If there could not yet be one miners' union, at least all unions should be tightly bound in an inclusive federation, and conversely the employers should be compelled to negotiate on a national basis. It was a development little to the taste of many of the smaller unions, and even less to the liking of employers, who, in mining and other industries, continued to insist on the dangers of making local considerations subordinate to the levelling doctrine of universality. The mining employers as a class were not noted for far-sightedness, but there was something in the argument. There was a danger that national juggernauts would crush local traditions and practices, and eliminate local autonomy, and that, once set in motion, even on behalf of a sectional aim, it would be very difficult to stop. The question was in fact already arising whether the big sprawling union would be the best method of dealing with labour demands.

The same issue arose in the case of the Transport Workers' Federation. In 1912, the docks industry again flared up. The Port of London Authority, and other port employers, would not recognise the Transport Workers' Federation, although they were prepared to deal with the local unions, and indeed the Federation had so far proved itself better able to foment a mass insurrection, than to control it. The issue of industrial unionism was at stake, and the Federation had intoxicating memories of the successes of 1911. The port of London was stopped over the employment of a non-union worker, and the Federation appealed for sympathetic action in other ports. The response was meagre, the Port of London Authority was adamant, and the strike collapsed ignominiously. This reverse was a shock to the militants and in particular to the Federation. It exposed the hollowness of the Federation's claim to be national, and taught the lesson, which had been inculcated in other unions a generation before, that progress depended on sheer organisation more than on inflammatory slogans.

It was on the railways, where community of workers' interests was apparent, and the number of employers was small, that industrial unionism achieved its most striking success at this juncture. The railway strike of 1911 had required solidarity, and in 1913 three of the unions amalgamated to form the National Union of Railwaymen, but the Associated Society of Locomotive Engineers and Firemen refused to join the merger, as did the Railway Clerks' Association. Generally, however, the attitude to amalgamation or to greater centralisation of the trade union movement as a whole was at best lukewarm, for both involved the surrender of independence in some degree.

The size of the trade union movement had greatly increased, but in the four years preceding the War, when it rose from 2½ million to over 4 million, the balance of power within it had substantially altered, as a result of the drive in the ranks of transport workers and general labourers. The growth of the 'new' unionism had not seriously affected the predominance of building and engineering craftsmen, cotton operatives, and coal-miners, who accounted in 1895 for some two-thirds of the total membership. Between 1910 and 1913, however, their proportion declined to less than one-half. The figure for the railways had almost doubled, and the total for transport, including sea-transport, and the fast-growing road-transport, had risen from 257,000 to 694,000, and came second only to that for coal-mining. The figure for general labourers showed an even sharper advance, from 81,000 to 358,000.[10]

Syndicalism predicated unity of action not only within each industry, but between industries. The Miners' Federation took the initiative in developing this policy. Its President, Robert Smillie, wrote that 'sympathetic action is no longer to be left to the uncontrolled emotions of a strike period, but is to be the calculated result of mature consideration and careful planning. The predominant idea of the alliance is that each of these great fighting organisations, before embarking upon any big movements, either defensive or aggressive, should formulate its programme, submit it to the others, and that upon joint proposals joint action should then be taken.'[11]

The alliance was the Triple Industrial Alliance forged between the Miners' Federation, the National Union of Railwaymen and the Transport Workers' Federation in 1914. It was designed to exert simultaneous pressures on the employers in furtherance of national claims, with a common strike if necessary. On the face of it, the Alliance, representing a total of some two million workers, presaged an extension and intensification of the industrial struggle, and a head-on clash between labour and the State. Whether the Alliance was as solid as it appeared remained for the time being unproved, for in August of the same year, the 'Kaiser's War' broke out.

The industrial strife had already, in 1912, prompted the

Government to set up the Industrial Council, equally representative of trade unions and employers, which was to settle
disputes referred to it, and to foster conciliation processes. The
Government hoped that disputants might have recourse to it
before declaring strikes or lock-outs, but both sides of industry
were suspicious of it from the start. The Council was also asked
to consider how best industrial agreements could be made to
work. Its Report, issued in 1913, pronounced against fines for
breach of agreements, or compulsory arbitration, which could
prejudice the principle of 'mutual consent', on which the existing machinery was based. It did suggest, however, that, where
deadlock between the parties occurred, 'in order that the interests of the community may be adequately safe-guarded', a
strike or lock-out should not take place until the issue in dispute
was pronounced on by some authority representing the interests of the community, in the form of an independent chairman. The Council was written off as a failure, because, according to its Chairman, the Chief Industrial Commissioner, Sir
George (later Lord) Askwith, among other weaknesses it had no
power to insist on disputes being brought to it or to enforce its
decisions, while its recommendations 'would have caught no
votes', and were disliked by the T.U.C., to which the Government referred them, as tending towards compulsory arbitration.
He was certainly right in asserting that the Government 'had
little or no labour policy', but that had been the case for some
two centuries. (It is worth mentioning that in 1924 Askwith got
a Bill through the House of Lords making a strike or lock-out
illegal, where the Ministry of Labour had remitted the dispute
in question to a court of inquiry under the Industrial Courts
Act.) [12]
Until the First War, therefore, the machinery for settling
disputes rested on the goodwill or good sense of the parties. By
the beginning of the war, most of the large industries had
evolved some sort of bargaining procedure, although the administration on both sides was still usually woefully inadequate.
In 1905 there were 162 conciliation and arbitration boards, and

by 1913 the number had almost exactly doubled (325).[13] The vast majority of disputes were being settled by negotiation, and a decreasing proportion by dictation.[14] Public opinion was no doubt partly responsible, for there was a growing feeling that force should be used only as a last resort, but the main reason was simply a recognition of facts; trades unions were there to stay, and, even if they were not, labour demands had to be considered. The smooth running of industry, and not any greater appreciation of the public need, demanded that there should be machinery of consultation between both sides. The trade unions were growing bigger partly because the units of management were also doing so. Joint-stock and limited liability were working along with a process of amalgamation to make for greater aggregations of capital, larger employers. Business was becoming a matter of departments, including labour departments. And the employers themselves were being linked more and more in associations, either for restrictive trading purposes, or, more frequently, for dealing on a common basis with trade unions.

REFERENCES

1. B. C. ROBERTS: *The Trades Union Congress (op. cit.)*, p. 258.
2. R. C. K. ENSOR: *op. cit.*, p. 515;
   Industrial Relations Handbook (Ministry of Labour), 1953.
3. *17th Abstract of Labour Statistics*, pp. 88, 102.
4. R. C. K. ENSOR: p. 502.
5. *Trade Union Documents*, ed. MILNE-BAILEY (Bell, 1929), pp. 74–5, 126.
6. *18th Abstract of Labour Statistics*, p. 173.
7. K. G. J. C. KNOWLES: *Strikes — A study in Industrial Conflict* (Blackwell, 1952), p. 8;
   B. C. ROBERTS: p. 234;
   J. SYMONS: *The General Strike* (Cresset Press, 1957), p. 51;
   S. and B. WEBB: pp. 655–8.
8. R. C. K. ENSOR: p. 440. For a trade union leader's views see *Churchill, by His Contemporaries* (Hutchinson, 1953), pp. 250–1.
9. B. C. ROBERTS: pp. 241–52.
10. G. D. H. COLE: *A Short History of the British Working-Class Movement* (Allen & Unwin, 1952), pp. 321–43;
    18th Abstract of Labour Statistics;

B. C. ROBERTS: *Trade Union Government and Administration in Great Britain* (London School of Economics and Political Science — Bell, 1957), App. I, pp. 479–84.

11. F. WILLIAMS: *Magnificent Journey* (Odhams Press, 1954), p. 280.

12. *Trade Union Documents*, p. 257;
LORD ASKWITH: *op. cit.*, pp. 180–2.

13. Committee on Industry and Trade: *Survey of Industrial Relations* (1926), p. 254. In 1894 there had been only 64. (*Annual Report of Labour Dept.*, Board of Trade, 1895.)

14. LORD AMULREE: *op. cit.*, pp. 288–9.

CHAPTER VII

TRADE UNIONS IN THE FIRST WORLD WAR

WHEN the War began, the labour situation was threatening. 'Its outbreak came at a time when disturbances in the ranks of British labour were more serious and wide-spread than they had been at any time since the rise of large-scale organisation,' wrote Lloyd George. 'The old industrial tyranny of the nine-teenth century was breaking up. A new and hopeful spirit of justifiable discontent was abroad, fostered by the spread of education. . . . Workers were agitating for a higher standard of life and a more dignified status than they had endured in the past. From 1911 onwards, there was a steady development of strike action, and in the summer of 1914 there was every sign that the autumn would witness a series of industrial disturb-ances without precedent. Trouble was threatening in the rail-way, mining, engineering and building industries. Disagree-ments were active, not only between employers and employed, but in the internal organisation of the workers. A strong "rank and file" movement, keenly critical of the policy and methods of the official leaders of Trade Unionism, had sprung up, and was gaining steadily in strength.'[1]

The War enormously enhanced the power and public pres-tige of the unions, and at the same time gave free play to the dissident elements within the movement.

This was a war of men and of materials on a scale never be-fore experienced or imagined, and it was a war in which the issue at stake was not the gain or loss of some distant territory, but the survival of Britain as a great power. It was a matter of life and death that the resources of the nation should be ex-ploited to the limit, and even beyond. Manpower must be deployed to the best advantage, both in industry and in the Forces, and, however effectively this was done, the time would come when it was a case of 'scraping the barrel'. Organised labour was still only half-conscious of its strength, but there could be no doubt in the minds of those who were alive to recent trends, that it was a gigantic force, which the government of a country in dire peril could not afford to ignore.

In their own rights as industrial organisations, the trade unions were in effect brought into the administration of government, and finally into the Government itself. This development owed little to party politics. The Labour Party's numerical strength in Parliament was small — a little over forty members — though the precise balance between Liberals and Conservatives gave it influence out of all proportion to its size. Once Liberals and Conservatives reached a working accord, however, in the first Coalition Government, Labour was reduced to its relative electoral stature.

The Labour Party, too, was weakened by internal differences over the rights and wrongs of the War and war policy. Those differences were to a great extent a manifestation of the different philosophies of the political socialists on the one hand, and the trade union representatives on the other. And there was no doubt which section would win if there were a clash. It was significant that, almost immediately, J. Ramsay MacDonald was replaced as leader of the Labour Party by the trade unionist M.P. Arthur Henderson (7th August, 1914). The Independent Labour Party might continue, as it did, to criticise the conduct of the War; what mattered much more to the Government was that the trade unions should give their support, and this they did whole-heartedly on all essential points. Arthur Henderson became a member of the Coalition Government, although he was not given Cabinet rank.

The 'Industrial Truce', called by the unions soon after hostilities began, was inspired partly by patriotism, partly by the common belief that the War would so disrupt industry as to precipitate large-scale unemployment, and that in any case it would be of short duration. In the event, a labour shortage of unparalleled intensity quickly materialised. Labour was invested with unprecedented bargaining power and it exercised it. As profits soared, so did wage-demands become more strident, backed by strikes. Many employers and many unions, reported the Industrial Commissioner, were 'openly exploiting the needs of the Nation'.[2] After the initial pause, the number of recorded stoppages swelled from ten at the beginning of 1915, to seventy-four in March of the same year. There were ugly strikes in the shipbuilding and engineering industries on the Clyde, partly political — the I.L.P. was strongly entrenched there — and partly in revolt against the 'Industrial Truce'.

It was imperative that the country should not be weakened and distracted, and the production of munitions retarded by labour unrest. The co-operation of the trade union leadership was essential, and it was willingly extended. In March, 1915, trade union spokesmen were summoned to consult with the Chancellor of the Exchequer and the President of the Board of Trade, whose department was responsible for labour affairs, on the measures to be taken. Here was a remarkable acknowledgment of labour's importance, and Lloyd George records the bewilderment of Balfour, invited to be present, as he saw, within the sacred sanctum of the Treasury, 'stalwart artisans . . . on equal terms negotiating with the Government of the day', and witnessed 'this sudden revelation of a new power'.[3]

The Government's aim was to avoid strikes through compulsory arbitration, and to get the unions to lift, for the duration of the War, their restrictions on output and on the use of semi-skilled and female labour in the munitions industries. This policy had been recommended by the Committee on Production, under the Chief Industrial Commissioner, after consultation with representatives of the trade unions and employers. The outcome of the Conference was the 'Treasury Agreement', which recorded understandings on both these points, coupled with a proviso that the manufacturers' profits in the industries concerned should be limited. The Amalgamated Society of Engineers signed a similar agreement a week later, although, naturally enough, it was not well disposed, as a craft union with long-established traditions of restriction, to the idea of 'dilution of labour'. A committee representative of the unions was to be established to advise the Government on labour matters, and the National Labour Advisory Council was duly constituted, under the chairmanship of Arthur Henderson.

The Treasury Agreements, which their chief architect, Lloyd George, regarded as 'opening up a great new chapter in the history of Labour in its relations with the State', were given statutory force in the Munitions of War Act (July, 1915), applying to establishments controlled by the State, but capable of extension to other vital industries. There was to be no strike or lock-out unless twenty-one days' notice had first been given to enable the Government to refer the dispute to an official agency; the Committee on Production was designated for this purpose. A dispute in an undertaking not scheduled could be brought within the scope of the Act by a Royal Proclamation. Profits were to be controlled, as well as wages and salaries. Restrictive practices were to be suspended, and there were controls on the movement of labour, through a system of 'leaving certificates', reminiscent of the Tudor device to control labour restlessness. The principle of dilution of labour was recognised.

The Act was only partially successful in subduing either the rapacity of a part of the employers, or the indiscipline of a part of labour. It did not allow for strikes against Government policy, which became more frequent as the War went on, nor could a declaration of illegality of itself prevent or end a strike. It had a sobering effect, however, and compulsory arbitration was a safety-valve. In 1915, nearly 3 million working days were lost by strikes, and $2\frac{1}{3}$ million in the following year, but these figures were low by pre-war standards; in 1913 and 1914 the figures had been around the 10 million mark.[4]

Significantly enough, the first major challenge to the principle of compulsory arbitration and the outlawing of strikes came from the miners. The Miners' Federation had openly rejected the principle so far as their own industry was concerned, and in July 1915 the South Wales Miners' Federation declared a strike, affecting about 200,000 men. It was proclaimed illegal, although the mines were not State-controlled at this stage, but the Government could not afford a trial of strength with the Federation, and used its influence to concede much of the strikers' claims. The motives of the leaders in this case were not above suspicion. They had refused to put away the strike weapon, and a national strike had been threatened earlier in the year. Syndicalism was strong. *The Miners' Next Step*, published in 1912, had denounced not only the capitalist structure, but the conception of state control favoured by most socialists; the State itself was to be overthrown by industrial action, and the workers were to take over.

Fortunately, union policy in general was in support of the war-effort, and as the War went on, so did Government bring the unions more fully into its counsels. When Lloyd George became Prime Minister, in 1916, he gave labour a place in the scheme of things which it had never had before. Henderson, who had previously been given Cabinet rank, and been made Labour Adviser to the Government, now became a member of the Inner Cabinet of five. The new Government created a Ministry of Labour from the consolidation of the Labour Departments of the Board of Trade and the Ministry of Munitions. Lloyd George appointed a trade unionist M.P., John Hodge, of the Steel Smelters, to be its head, and he made another trade union official, George Barnes, of the Amalgamated Society of Engineers, head of the new Ministry of Pensions. J. R. Clynes became Parliamentary Secretary of the Ministry of Food, and later Food Controller. A Ministry of National Service was formed. The Government's measures also included the extension of State control to mines and shipping.

Incidentally, Lloyd George's policy of allying organised labour with the Government, and his percipience in recognising talent, were strikingly illustrated by his invitation in 1917 to

Ernest Bevin, of the Dockers' Union, to accept a Government post as labour adviser. This was also an extraordinary case of coming events casting their shadows far before.[5]

Although the Labour Party Executive decided by a majority of only one to accept the invitation to take part in the Government, altogether eight Labour men were given office. Trade Unions were given representation (with employers and Government) on the Cotton and Wool Control Boards; that is, they were allotted a share in the control of industry. The trade union leadership as a whole, although it had its anti-war elements to contend with, remained much more solidly in support of the war effort than did the Labour politicians. A striking manifestation of the divergence between the workers' and the politicians' approach was the refusal, in 1917, of the Sailors' and Firemen's Union — bitterly and with reason anti-German — to permit Ramsay MacDonald to sail to Russia in connection with an international conference of Socialists.

Much the greater part of the industrial unrest during the War was attributable to the work of unofficial leaders. The trade unions' close association with Governmental measures automatically made them suspect to many of their members. These measures were deliberately repressive of freedom of industrial action, and in other directions, too, as with the issue of dilution of labour, went contrary to orthodox union policy. The union leaders were accused by the malcontents of having abandoned the tradition of militancy, and thus having become parties to reaction. There was, too, resentment of conscription for the Forces, introduced in 1916, in the working of which the trade unions were consulted by the Government.

The unions had been under fire from vociferous sections of their membership even before the War. It was alleged that the movement was suffering from inertia, and that this was largely due to the failure to adjust the structure and policy of trade unionism to modern needs. There was some truth in the charge. Unions had proliferated, without a common design, either in form or in policy, with the result that the movement was a

hotch-potch of organisations, often with machinery of the most
cumbrous type, and often encroaching on each other's territory
in a way frustrating not only to themselves but to the employers concerned. The movement towards industrial unionism
had made comparatively little headway since the establishment
of the N.U.R. in 1913. The T.U.C. was run on a financial shoe-
string, and represented organisations jealous of their independence, and often distrustful of each other, and was not likely to
give a lead. The sustained and bitter jealousy of the miners in
particular had reduced the G.F.T.U. to a comparatively insignificant rôle. The N.U.R., the Transport Workers' Federation, and the Miners' Federation had, as already seen, in 1914
formed the Triple Alliance, a bloc for the purpose of putting
irresistible pressure on employers in support of their respective
demands, through concerted strikes. The movement was once
again losing its impetus, and those who clamoured for reform
were looked at askance, not without reason; for the mass of
trade unionists had no desire to be used for political purposes,
and this was precisely what the syndicalists — and many of the
socialists — had in mind.[6]

There was ample scope for agitation in the mass of workers,
many of poor calibre — for the Services drained away a great
proportion of the best men — and many more bemused by
events, and irritated by the shortages and frustrations of civil
life. The situation immediately threw into prominence the shop
stewards. Shop stewards originally were a sort of non-commis-
sioned officers of the engineering trade unions, playing a minor
rôle in the works, with no executive powers. With the increase
of local labour problems, especially those arising from dilution,
they assumed on their own initiative an undue authority, which
was enhanced by the inadequacies of trade union machinery,
including the shortage of local officers, and by the remoteness
of union leaders preoccupied with national policies. The shop
stewards became the spokesmen of their workshop mates, de-
ferring less and less to the trade unions of which they were
nominally the delegates. They formed their own workshop

committees, and made contact with those in other workshops. A shop steward movement, more or less independent, developed, akin to the 'rank and file' movement which had harassed the unions before the war, and marked by sympathy with Industrial Unionism. It first showed its potentialities in 1915, on the Clyde, where Industrial Unionism had had many adherents before the War. An unofficial strike was declared, and a Central Withdrawal of Labour Committee set up to run it. The strike ended, but the Committee carried on, as the Clyde Workers' Committee, an association cutting horizontally across orthodox union boundaries, and hostile to orthodox union policies. Its spokesmen found political allies in the British Socialist Party and the Independent Labour Party, which were opposed to the continuance of the War. In 1916, the Committee led another Clydeside strike, so serious that some of the leaders were deported from the district. 'Shop Steward committees' and 'works committees' spread to other districts and other industries, and built up an organisation known as the National Workers' Committee Movement. The movement had always had a political complexion and the Russian Revolution in 1917 gave it a deeper tinge. It held national conferences in that year; in the third, seventy-two towns were represented. The number of strikes markedly increased, and the deterioration in the industrial situation became progressively worse. In 1917, nearly six million working-days were lost, more than double the previous year's total. There were rumours of a general strike, to be fomented by the I.L.P. and the so-called Union of Democratic Control. A conference was called by the I.L.P. and the British Socialist Party in June 'to hail the Russian Revolution, and to organise British Democracy to follow Russia'. It called for the establishment of Councils of Workmen's and Soldiers' Delegates, and proposed 'that the conveners of this Conference be appointed a Provisional Committee to implement the Conference's policy'.[7]

The Government appointed a Commission of eight persons on Labour Unrest, under George Barnes, which without much

G

difficulty discovered natural causes of discontent, not least
workers' loss of confidence in union leaders, and recommended
various ameliorative measures, including the adoption of the
Whitley Report, and the abolition of the system of leaving
certificates. Wage-grievances, especially among craftsmen, were
of course, an irritant, but the Government control of a large
part of industry, and of food prices, and the fact that there was
one national body, the Committee on Production, with a responsibility for wage settlements in one major sector, made it
possible to attempt a sort of overall wages-policy, roughly related to the cost of living. The system of guaranteed prices in
agriculture was accompanied by a system of wage-fixing
through the National Agricultural Wages Board. All this meant
a virtual suspension of ordinary collective bargaining over a
considerable section of the national economy, and its replacement by central regulation. It meant, too, that the tendency to
deal with labour matters on a national scale in particular industries was being given great encouragement. This development was facilitated by an Act (1917) making easier the procedure for amalgamation of trade unions.

The Whitley Reports were the work of the Committee
on the Relations between Employers and Employed —
itself a sub-committee of the Committee on Reconstruction. It
included trade union representatives and in its findings reflected the apprehension of trade union leaders about the
growth of the shop stewards' movement. In an Interim Report
in 1917, it recommended, for industries already well-organised,
'the establishment for each industry of an organisation, representative of employers and workpeople, to have as its object the
regular consideration of matters affecting the progress of the
trade from the point of view of all those engaged in it, so far as
this is consistent with the general interest of the community' —
that is, a Joint Standing Industrial Council, with District
Councils and Works Committees. The object was 'to secure
co-operation by granting to workpeople a greater share in
matters affecting their industry', such matters to include not

merely the adjustment of differences between the parties, but the utilisation of workpeople's practical knowledge, the promotion of security of employment, technical education and research, the improvement of processes and organisation, and industrial legislation. With the shop stewards' movement in mind, the Report declared that representation on the joint bodies must be through trade unions and employers' associations. Much importance was attached to the Works Committees, in which higher management should participate.

In spite of its composition, the Committee was looked at with suspicion by many in the trade union movement, and its recommendations were received with little enthusiasm in some quarters. The miners in particular rejected the principle on which it was based, that good relations between employers and workers were possible, as 'absolutely subversive to the aspirations of the workers and the proper development of the Trade Union movement'. The Parliamentary Committee of the T.U.C., when the Ministry of Labour passed the first Report to it, refused to give it any positive endorsement, and although it later recommended the acceptance of the principles of the Reports, it refrained from any detailed discussion of them. The fact was that, apart from Industrial Unionism, there was still the divergence between the old well-established craft unions, and the new general unions, seeking to build themselves up, as to the wisdom of having the State interfere in any way in the sphere of industrial relations.[8]

The recommendations were, however, accepted by both sides of industry, and by the Government, which indicated that the Councils would be accepted by it as 'Consultative Committees to the Government', playing 'a definite and permanent part in the economic life of the country'.

The Report gave a great and immediate impetus to the establishment of joint consultative machinery, and some seventy-three councils were set up in industry and civil administration, as well as thirty-three Interim Reconstruction Committees. A proportion of these lapsed after a time, but in

1927 they existed in fifty-four industries, representing some three million workpeople, and proved very effective in helping to keep the peace. The idea of Works Committees was much less popular, both with employers and trade unions, as potentially threatening to the functions of management and unions, while the Councils and their local off-shoots were primarily, though not always exclusively, occupied with the determination of wages and conditions, with comparatively little room allowed for the wider responsibilities advocated in the Report.[9]

The Committee produced five Reports in all. It recommended that industries lacking organisation of their own should be covered by an extension of the Trade Boards system, which was done by an Act of 1918. By 1921 there were sixty-three trade boards.

The fourth Report rejected utterly the adoption as a peace-time measure of compulsory arbitration, or the enforced delay of strikes and lock-outs pending investigation, as practised in Canada under the Lemieux Act, and recommended by the Industrial Council in 1913. Government had abandoned the prohibition of strikes and compulsory arbitration at the end of 1918, although it continued a measure of control over minimum rates of pay with the Wages (Temporary Regulation) Act of that year. The Committee advised instead the provision of effective machinery for voluntary arbitration, with authority for the Minister of Labour to inquire into particular disputes.

This recommendation was given effect in the Industrial Courts Act, 1919. The Act set up a standing Industrial Court, appointed by the Minister of Labour, and having an independent element, including the president, in addition to representatives of employers and workers. Under the Act, a dispute may be referred for settlement by the Court or other arbitration body only if both parties agree to this course. The Court's awards are not legally binding, so that the only compulsion behind them is of a moral kind. In eschewing compulsory arbitration, Britain rejected the example of the Dominions, Germany and the United States, and of other countries which were experimenting with legislation designed in various ways to curb strikes in the vital services. 'It was clearly contemplated that the Government might have to take some risks in permitting temporary industrial troubles to arise for the sake of making both sides face their responsibilities'.[10]

It appears that the original aim of the Ministry of Labour, in sponsoring such legislation, was a permanent court which would 'take a comprehensive view of the Labour question, and in particular . . . of the wages question', and so avoid what in fact did happen, 'a series of dissociated judgments'. In short, the Court was to have a wages policy of a sort. In the first draft of the Act, too, an element of compulsion was included, but it was withdrawn in deference to the protests of the trade unions, which were resolutely opposed to compulsory arbitration in any form.[11]

Under the Act, the Minister may, at his own discretion, where the public interest is involved, appoint a court of inquiry to report, 'not only in order that the dispute may be narrowed and clarified, but also to bring home the concern of the public, *i.e.* the consumer'. The direct interest of the community in industrial quarrels was thus given a diffident recognition.[12]

Throughout this period, the trade union movement became quantitatively stronger. In 1914 it had over four million members; between then and 1918, the membership rose by over one-half. Employers' associations, too, increased, and improved their organisation, and in 1916 one national body, the Federation of British Industries, was set up to protect the interests of employers as a whole, including their labour interests, in the light of the national trends in industrial relations and increasing Governmental interference. The old Employers' Parliamentary Association disappeared.

In doing this, the employers showed a greater awareness than the unions of the need for a body which would formulate and present a national policy, so far as this was practicable, and not be simply a lobbying agency. The T.U.C.'s central body was still the Parliamentary Committee, established in 1869; and although it had preserved its independence of the Labour Representation Committee and the Labour Party, its original functions and its nomenclature had obviously become out of date with the growth of direct labour representation in Parliament. It was, however, for want of a better the only body which could claim to speak for organised labour. In 1899 it had deliberately denied itself executive functions by setting up the General Federation of Trades Unions. This might have developed into an instrument for co-ordinating union policy, but in fact was never representative of the movement, and was never invested with the requisite authority to act on behalf of the movement. In 1916, the Miners and the N.U.R. succeeded in depriving it of even the semblance of partnership with the T.U.C., when it was ousted from the Joint Board representing the industrial and political wings of labour.[13]

In 1917, the T.U.C. demanded a part in the international work hitherto the prerogative of the G.F.T.U., and it was clearly only a matter of time before it insisted on the exclusive right of representation. The T.U.C., in short, was out to restrict the Federation to the functions of a benefit-paying society only, and even in this narrow sphere the latter's existence was precarious.[14] The war of attrition against the G.F.T.U. was not simply a struggle for power between two bodies operating in the same territory. The Federation clung to the old trade union traditions; it was essentially non-political, but in its political sympathies it was closer to the Liberals than to the Labour Party. The war, however, had disrupted the Liberal Party. The political labour movement, on the other hand, had been greatly strengthened by the War, and had seen new vistas of power opening up before it.

There was already talk in the T.U.C. of the need to improve its machinery to enable it to cope with its new and increasing responsibilities. There was still no certainty that the trade union movement would identify itself permanently with the Labour Party, for it was not only in the G.F.T.U. that this policy was looked at doubtfully. A dockers' delegate could affirm at the 1918 T.U.C. that he and most of his members were non-socialist. Havelock Wilson and other Lib-Lab survivors could and did still advocate a definite break between the T.U.C. and the Party. All this, however, was the manifestation of the wide-spread distrust in trade union ranks of socialism as a tenet, rather than a rejection of a workers' party. The Liberals had failed to make effective use in elections of working-class candidates. They were now torn by internal dissension. The Representation of the People Act of 1918 had given the vote to all men over twenty-one, and all women over thirty. The Labour Party saw its opportunity, and in 1918 adopted a new constitution and a positive programme designed to win popular support. Both were designed with an eye on the trade unions. The programme was more advanced than many trade unionists wanted, in its long-term objectives, but in its immediate aims it was the logical development of radicalism. The constitution fused the hitherto loosely-knit party structure into a national organisation, but care was taken to give the unions a majority of seats on the Executive, much to the disgust of the Independent Labour Party. Thus, although there might be, and was, active dissent on the part of both the right wing and the left wing of the labour movement, the foundations were laid of a solid alliance between the industrial and political organisations. The misery and frustration of the post-war industrial depression were to give it ample stimulus and opportunity.[15]

The War had imposed restraints on both sides of industry, but each was anxious to be rid of them so far as they inhibited them in the exercise of particular rights and privileges. The War had done little towards a permanent improvement of relations between the parties, and indeed a trial of strength was almost inevitable. The employers on the one hand were jealous of State interference, and of the status the emergency had conferred on labour. The unions, on the other hand, had enlarged not only their power, but their ideas, and were confident that with peace would come the opportunity for advance on a broad front.

REFERENCES

1. D. LLOYD GEORGE: *War Memoirs* (Odhams Press, 1938), II, pp. 1141–2. Industrial unrest reached its peak in 1912, and thereafter subsided.
2. *Ibid.*, I, p. 180.
3. *Ibid.*, I, pp. 176–7.
4. H. M. D. PARKER: 'Manpower' (*History of Second World War*), (H.M.S.O., 1957), p. 9.
5. TREVOR EVANS: *Bevin* (Allen & Unwin, 1946), p. 69.
6. COLE and POSTGATE: *op. cit.*, pp. 484–95.
7. D. LLOYD GEORGE: II, p. 1154.
8. B. C. ROBERTS: *The Trades Union Congress*, pp. 290–1; *Trade Union Documents*, pp. 494–6.
9. D. LLOYD GEORGE: II, pp. 1161–2; *Trade Union Documents*, pp. 496–501; *Survey of Industrial Relations* (*op. cit.*), p. 45; G. D. H. COLE: *op. cit.*, pp. 368–9.
10. *Survey of Industrial Relations*, p. 263.
11. LORD AMULREE: *op. cit.*, p. 173; G. D. H. COLE: p. 394.
12. *Survey of Industrial Relations*, p. 48.
13. B. C. ROBERTS: p. 283.
14. *Ibid.*, p. 295.
15. *Ibid.*, pp. 303–4.

CHAPTER VIII

TRADE UNIONS AND THE DEPRESSION

IN the immediate post-war period (1919–20), the omens were indeed propitious for labour. There was a relaxation of effort, on the part of both management and labour, which was partly a natural reaction, but was in no small degree induced by the high prices and high wages which resulted from the release of long-pent commodity demands. Both employers and workers were reluctant to accept the need of adjustment to a peace-time economy, and for a while the artificial boom disguised it only too well.

The Labour Party's electoral expectations were disappointed in the first post-war election, but political frustration as usual served only to divert activity into industrial channels. Although much of this activity was unofficial, and a source of worry to trade union leaders, the trade unions were on the crest of the wave. Their membership rose between 1918 and 1920 from six and a half millions to eight and one-third millions. There was a move towards strengthening their organisation, especially by contraction and fusion, which had been facilitated by the Trade Union (Amalgamation) Act of 1917. A notable feature was the creation of large-scale general unions, the Transport and General Workers' Union and the National Union of General and Municipal Workers, which concentrated on the recruitment of the hitherto ill-organised unskilled workers.

In the flush of post-war prosperity, the unions adopted a militant policy, with demands for shorter hours and higher wages, enforced by strikes. In the van was the Miners' Federation, which had as an essential part of its programme the public ownership of the mines, with democratic control, which meant that the workers themselves should have a decisive say in the running of the industry. This programme was put forward early in 1919, supported by the threat of an industry-wide stoppage, and was backed by the other members of the Triple Alliance, now again girding itself for action. The Government responded by appointing a Royal Commission on the Coal Industry (the Sankey Commission), and by summoning a National Joint Industrial Conference, intended to be representative of employers and unions. The members of the Triple Alliance, as well as the newly-formed Amalgamated Engineering Union, refused to be party to the Conference. Ernest Bevin, of the Transport and General Workers, expressed their attitude when he denounced the Conference as an attempt by the Government to seek to evade the issues dividing employers and workers. These differences, he held, could be resolved only by a trial of strength between the parties. The boycott gravely impaired the authority of the Conference. It duly presented recommendations, including the establishment of a National Joint Industrial Council, and the statutory enforcement of a forty-eight-hour week, already common in the better-organised industries. The Government declared its acceptance of these in principle, but little progress was made in implementing them, and the Conference finally collapsed with the withdrawal of the labour representatives.

A memorandum tabled by the union members of the Joint Committee of the Conference, setting out the 'Causes and Remedies for Labour Unrest', gave a clear indication of trade union views. 'With increasing vehemence,' it stated, 'Labour is challenging the whole structure of capitalist industry as it now exists. . . . It demands a system of industrial control which shall be truly democratic in character.' It cited the campaigns of the miners and railwaymen as illustrative of the 'demand of workers for a real share in industrial control', and asserted that 'the fundamental causes of Labour unrest are to be found rather in the growing determination of labour to challenge the whole existing structure of capitalist industry than in any of the more special and small grievances'. It admitted that the changes must be gradual, but insisted that private profit must go, and that labour had 'grown too strong to remain within the bounds of the old industrial system'.[1]

Here was evidence that in a fairly short space of time the orthodox trade union attitude had materially altered. It had been opposed to the view of Industrial Unionists and Syndicalists that a radical change in the whole structure of industry was necessary to the emancipation of the workers, and the trade union movement had indeed been condemned by the Industrial Workers of the World as being 'organised upon the basis of the identity of interests of the exploited and exploiting classes'.[2] Following the War, the shop steward movement lost its cohesion, but many of its ideas had infiltrated into the unions. There was a revival of the 'rank and file' element, which later blossomed into the Minority Movement. In the year of its inception (1924), it claimed to speak for 200,000 workers, and in 1925 for nearly one million. It was certainly strong enough to make trouble for the official leadership, and to ensure that the policy-makers took account of the kind of thinking it represented.[3] The militants were greatly stimulated by the disillusionment of the depression which began to settle on industry in the latter part of 1920, since the capitalist system appeared quite incapable of coping with the disastrous recession in trade.

The trade union leaders, who, before the War, with some exceptions, had been at best half-hearted about socialism, were becoming more and more convinced that a drastic reform of the industrial structure was essential. They were, too, becoming converted to the view, long cherished by the more extreme elements, that this could be achieved only by industrial action of a concerted kind.

1919 was a troubled year, and the main centre of unrest was again the mining industry. The miners' leaders' own solution of their troubles was simple, if drastic: to expropriate all mine-owners, to vest the operation of the industry in a Mining Council, half of whose members would be appointed by the Government, the other half by the Miners' Federation, and to give the

Council power to take over associated activities, including shipping. They did not, however, confine themselves to industrial grievances. Just before the Sankey Commission was appointed, they were demanding of the T.U.C. a trade union challenge, in the form of strike action, to the Government's attitude to Russia and to certain domestic issues, and, although they failed wholly to persuade the T.U.C., they gained the support of the other members of the Triple Alliance.

The composition of the Sankey Commission was such as to make disagreement almost a foregone conclusion. The Miners' Federation had successfully insisted on six members directly or indirectly representative of labour; three represented the employers and three were Government nominees, in addition to the Chairman. The Chairman's report, advocating nationalisation of the industry, was supported in principle by the labour members, and dissented from by the rest, although one suggested a form of public regulation. The Government pleaded that the Commission had failed to produce a policy, and was furiously assailed by the miners and their allies, and threatened with the displeasure of the T.U.C.

In September, the National Union of Railwaymen called a national strike against proposed wage reductions, said by the Companies to be in line with the fall in the cost of living, and there were broad hints, from an extemporised trade union 'Mediation Committee' that, failing a settlement, the stoppage would spread to other industries. The Government made arrangements for the transport of essential supplies, but an agreement was quickly reached. A special meeting of the T.U.C., in December, 1919, was held to consider the miners' demand for a general strike in support of nationalisation of their industry; but the employment situation had improved, and feeling had abated; the T.U.C. merely agreed to promote a political campaign in favour of the miners' cause.

Events, and not least the emergence of the unofficial 'Mediation Committee', were demonstrating that the trade union movement needed a central executive body with more authority than that possessed by the Parliamentary Committee of the T.U.C. At the December session, it was agreed that the Parliamentary Committee should be abolished, and replaced by a General Council, with power to co-ordinate policy in major disputes. The General Council was eventually constituted, but with the all-important proviso that 'the complete autonomy' of the affiliated unions should remain unimpaired.[4]

In the same year, the National Confederation of Employers' Organisations took over from the Federation of British Industries responsibility for the co-ordination of employers' labour policies. Both sides of industry were marshalling their forces.

The threat of a general strike was only in abeyance. It was used again in 1920 as a means of dissuading the Government from intervening in support of Poland in the latter's campaign against Russia. A joint conference of the Labour Party and the T.U.C. agreed on this policy, and Ernest Bevin, who had already given official sanction to a refusal by dockers to load an arms shipment for Poland, led a delegation to the Prime Minister to warn the Government. A Council of Action to organise the strike was set up, but the Russo-Polish war died down, and the emergency passed.[5]

A fresh mining dispute in the same year revived the possibility of widespread sympathetic stoppages. The miners declared a national strike, and invoked the help of the Triple Alliance. Although in the event this help was refused, the Government was moved to pass the Emergency Powers Act, 'for securing the essentials of life to the community'. It was designed in case of action taken or threatened 'of such a nature and on so extensive a scale as to be calculated, by interfering with the supply and distribution of food, water, fuel or light, or with the means of locomotion, to deprive the community, or any substantial portion of the community, of the essentials of life'. The Government was empowered in such circumstances to declare a state of emergency, and take appropriate measures with Parliament's approval. There was to be no compulsory service or industrial conscription, and the right to strike was not prejudiced. The Bill was not seriously challenged by the trade union movement, although it was condemned by Ernest Bevin and others.

The depression deepened, and the Government hurried to divest itself of its industrial controls. The mining industry was freed in 1921, as were, a little later in the year, the railways. The miners, faced as a result with the loss of their cherished system of national wage regulation, as well as with wage-cuts, rose in revolt. They again invoked the help of the Triple Alliance, and this time the response was favourable. The three great unions agreed on complete stoppages in their industries, and the Government retorted by declaring a state of emergency. Negotiations took place, and at the last minute the strike was postponed. The Miners' Executive rejected proposals for a temporary settlement of the wages issue alone, apparently against the advice of its Secretary, Frank Hodges, and the other two unions in the alliance withdrew their support. Not for the last time, the intransigence of the Miners' Federation, as it appeared even to their allies, defeated the design of concerted action. Clearly, if there was to be any sort of General Staff, the commanders of each of the armies in the field must defer to Headquarters. The Alliance collapsed, and the date was called, in labour circles, 'Black Friday'. After a protracted stoppage on their own, the miners gave way.

Unemployment rose throughout industry, and wages fell, as did trade union funds and memberships. There were bitter disputes, notably one in the engineering industry, which centred on the employers' insistence that their managerial functions, as they understood them, were no business of the union. The total of lost working days in 1921 swelled to nearly 86 millions, more than double the pre-war record of 1912 (41 millions). As the trade unions floundered in the depression, and industrial militancy declined, so once again there was a swing of labour towards political action. In the 1922 General Election, the Labour Party vastly increased its Parliamentary strength, (59 to 142), and in 1923 returned with no less than 191 members. With the help of the Liberals, the first Labour Government was formed in 1924. There was, however, no abatement of labour unrest during its brief existence, and only a speedy ending to the railway strike of that year prevented recourse to the Emergency Powers Act. The Government's emergency organisation, set up, under a Civil Commission, to operate supply and transport services, was not called on, and was allowed to lapse. It was highly significant, however, that the Government, and the first Labour Government at that, should make preparations against a large-scale strike.[6]

The improvement of trade in 1924 proved short-lived, and the struggle between employers and workers gained a new intensity. The coal-mines again became the cockpit of industry, for the employers, hard-hit by the fall in coal prices — many mines were working at a loss — were demanding cheaper production through lower wages and longer hours. Again in 1925 the T.U.C., alarmed by the implied threat to workers in general, promised support for the miners, to the point of sympathetic industrial action, and its special committee met the Prime Minister; and again the Government — this time a powerful Conservative Government, for the Labour Government had not long survived — staved off the 'showdown' by giving a temporary subsidy and appointing another Royal Commission.

The Samuel Commission was very differently constituted from the Sankey Commission, lacking a miners' bloc, or indeed any direct labour representation, and its recommendations, which appeared in March, 1926, were more modest and coherent: nationalisation only of royalties, re-organisation of the industry and wage reductions. These were unpalatable, in whole or in part, to owners and workers alike, and were rejected outright by the latter, and there was stalemate. The employers gave notice of the termination of the existing contracts, and tabled proposals which certainly the miners would not accept. Negotiations, with which the Prime Minister was associated, proved abortive. The miners asked the T.U.C. to implement its earlier promise of support, and a conference of trade union executives agreed on a general strike. It was not a 'snap' decision; as early as January, the Industrial Committee of the T.U.C. had considered what would be the most effective form of sympathetic action, and had reaffirmed its whole-hearted support for the miners against any reduction in wages, increase of hours, or interference with national agreements.[7]

The Government was already alerted to the explosive possibilities of the situation; it could hardly be otherwise, having regard to the trend of events in the past few years, and to the experience of its immediate predecessors. Already, in 1925, it had set up an Emergency Committee on Supply and Transport, under the able guidance of John Anderson, then Permanent Under-Secretary to the Home Office, which by the end of the year had worked out a scheme. The circular to Local Authorities, outlining it, stated that 'the events of recent years have shown that an industrial dispute may be so extended as to interfere seriously with communications, the conveyance of food and other necessities, the supply of light and power and the health and means of livelihood of the population at large'. While governmental authorities, local and national, should 'keep aloof' from industrial disputes as such, the protection of the community in an 'emergency' was essential. Accordingly, regional organisations were to be set up, with the requisite powers.[8]

The Prime Minister, Baldwin, struck a warning note on the same theme: 'If the will to strike should overcome the will to peace temporarily . . . no minority in a free country has ever yet coerced the community. . . . If the time should come when the community has to protect itself, with the strength of the Government behind it, the community will do so.' A section of the community had, in 1925, independently of the Government, envisaged the need for preparedness, and had started an unofficial agency, the Organisation for the Maintenance of Supplies, for the recruitment of volunteer workers in case of a national stoppage.[9]

On the other side — for it was already clear that in threatening a general strike the unions were challenging not only the
mine-owners, but the Government — were the miners' officials
and their associates. Whether they had weighed the full implications of a general strike is doubtful, but certainly it was not
for want of time or opportunity; some of the leaders had for
long reflected on its use. The Secretary of the Miners' Federation, A. J. Cook, had often proclaimed his extreme views, in
speech and writing; he boasted that he didn't 'care a fig for any
Government, or army, or navy', and earlier had declared that
the T.U.C. was the Parliament of the future. His President,
Herbert Smith, was said to be obstinate to the point of stupid-
ity, and convinced that the capitalist system was on the point of
disintegration.[10] Ernest Bevin had foreseen the need, and the
occasion, for a better integration of the trade union movement
when, in the previous year, he had proposed a new and broader
Industrial Alliance, to enforce union demands, in the last resort, by a strike so damaging to the community that the Government must become involved in the struggle; and while this project had not had time to materalise, there were other union
leaders similarly inclined. The railwaymen twice since the war
had not hesitated to declare national strikes — and railways
were still the main artery of transport and supply. The Communist Party, its appeal enhanced by the Russian Revolution,
the collapse of the shop steward movement after the war, and
the depression, was strong in the mines. On the labour side, the
dislike of a general strike was most evident among the politicians, who stood to gain little, if anything, from it, since its success would upset the balance between the industrial and the
political forces, just when it was going in favour of the political
side, and its failure would be bound to discredit the labour
movement as a whole.

On April 30th, 1926, the negotiations broke down, and the
Government drafted a Proclamation of a State of Emergency,
which was published next day. A scheme for a stoppage of work,
already prepared, was approved by a Conference of Union

H

Secretaries on the following day by a large majority, and the same afternoon strike notices were sent out. It appears the Government was not then aware of this last development, and the Industrial Committee of the Unions was invited to meet members of the Cabinet that evening to seek a solution. The talks continued on the next day (Sunday), but broke down on the miners' outright rejection of any wage reductions. Negotiations between representatives of the T.U.C. General Council and the Government were broken off on May 3rd, but not simply because the printing staff in the *Daily Mail* offices had refused to produce a leading article on the situation to which they objected. The Government made this 'gross interference with the freedom of the press' a complaint, but its main grievance appeared to be that the unions, even while the negotiations were in progress, had sent out instructions to their members 'in several of the most vital industries of the country to carry out a general strike' on the following Tuesday. The Government demanded, as a condition of the resumption of negotiations, that the strike notices should be withdrawn, and that the Trade Union Committee should repudiate the printers' action. The Unions' reply was evasive. It did not deny the first and most serious charge, and commented somewhat blandly that 'it is nothing unusual for workmen to cease work in defence of their interests as wage-earners', the motive this time being to support the miners. It professed ignorance of the printers' actions. Not surprisingly, the Government found the reply unsatisfactory, if not downright provocative, and the negotiations were terminated. The strike began, with about one and a quarter million men immediately involved. Ernest Bevin became one of the two chief organisers.[11]

There has been some debate as to whether the General Strike was illegal, or was even 'general'. The latter argument rests on no better premise than that the strike was confined to certain vital industries, which is tantamount to saying that a battle is not general because the commander does not immediately deploy the whole of his forces. As for the other point, while the

question whether it would rank as a sympathetic strike and so be
quite legitimate, is interesting, the real issue is whether it was
directed, in part at least, against the Government. In their
strike instructions, the unions had specifically associated the
Government with the mine-owners as the instigators of a lock-
out, and clearly implied that their attack was directed partly, if
not mainly, against it. It seems obvious, in light of the industrial
history of the previous few years, that the intention of the strike
was to coerce the Government, in the first place, for a certain
purpose, namely, the satisfaction of the miners' demands. So far
as the Government could be said to be involved, the opinion of
Mr. Justice Astbury (in an action by the National Sailors' and
Firemen's Union to restrain one of its branches from calling out
its members) was that the strike must be illegal since 'no trade
dispute does or can exist between the T.U.C. on the one hand,
and the Government and the nation on the other'. This presumably would deprive the strikers of the legal immunity given
by the Trade Disputes and the Conspiracy and Protection of
Property Acts.[12]

The strike was a failure, and was bound to be, and indeed
there were friends of labour and probably some of the leaders
who hoped it would be. For instance, C. T. Cramp, of the
National Union of Railwaymen, at the T.U.C. National Strike
Special Conference held in January 1927, while acknowledging that his was a minority view, said: 'I do not believe in a
general strike. I have never believed in a general strike to
achieve something positive, though I believe it could be used
to negative something which might be thrust upon this nation
... you cannot have a general strike without hitting your own
people first, and trying to carry it out to its logical conclusion
means that you get absolutely nowhere ... the time for a
general strike to be effective has long gone by in a highly
organised country like ours.' [13] Beatrice Webb said its success
'would mean that a militant minority were starving the majority into submission to their will, and would be the end of democracy, industrial as well as political'; but of course she did not

favour 'the pernicious doctrine of "workers" control'.[14] The Liberal Asquith called the strike 'the coercion of a new dictatorship', and condemned the method as 'the most deadly menace to representative government'.[15]

The General Strike was estimated to have cost the country thirty million pounds. It ended in unconditional defeat for the trade union movement, for its leaders received no guarantees as condition of their capitulation. They had challenged not only the Government, but, as Baldwin had said, the community, and the strength and the feelings of the community were too strong for them. The forces of the Government were shrewdly used, under the Emergency Powers Act, but the first shock assault of the unions had failed to paralyse or terrify the country, and they could not hope to win a war of attrition. Their resolution evaporated, except in the case of the miners' leaders, who stubbornly contrived to fight, alone, a tragic and hopeless battle for another six months.

The collapse of the General Strike was a body-blow to the whole trade union movement. It was a well-nigh fatal blow to the syndicalist school. It appeared that its ultimate sanction, the general strike, so long regarded by its critics as well as its exponents as the ultimate and decisive weapon, would shatter itself against the solidity of a well entrenched government, and a divided public opinion. The defeat made a deep and abiding psychological impression on the leaders and their membership which, combined with the deepening industrial depression, forced the abandonment for a time of the policy of militancy.[16]

In 1927 the Government followed up its victory with the Trade Disputes and Trade Union Act. It forbade strikes, including sympathetic strikes (and lock-outs), 'designed or calculated to coerce the Government either directly or by inflicting hardship on the community'. (Sympathetic strikes as such were not forbidden.) The Act of 1913 relating to trade union funds was amended so that a member, instead of being required to 'contract out' of his subscription to his union's political fund, was now to be free of this obligation unless he signed a special form to the contrary, 'contracting in'. Civil servants' unions must not be affiliated to the T.U.C. Local authorities were debarred from making union membership a condition of service. Picketing was made subject to new restrictions. No doubt with the extension of public services in mind, the Act made it an offence for a person employed by a local or other public authority wilfully to break his contract of service, 'knowing or having reasonable cause to believe that the probable consequences of his so doing, either alone or in combination with others, will be to cause injury or danger or grave inconvenience to the community'. [17]

The trade unions would not rest until the 1927 Act was repealed. The Act was ambiguous in its phrasing, for the draughtsmen had not overcome the ancient difficulty of defining adequately the boundaries between the legitimate province of the trade unions and the province of the State. For instance, any sympathetic strike was liable to inflict hardship on the community, and might therefore be adjudged an attack on the Government. The Act was, of course, intended to deprive trade unions of a part of their powers and privileges, and was bitterly resented on that score. It was also regarded by the unions as a stigma on their movement, the mark of a humiliating failure, particularly, of course, by those most closely identified with it. Its removal would require a Labour Government, since it was unlikely that a Conservative Government would revoke it. A Labour Government was not long delayed, for at the 1929 General Election the Conservatives were deposed, but it lacked an over-all majority. In 1930 it introduced a Bill to amend the Trade Disputes Act, by restoring 'contracting out' and certain other freedoms; but, although it received a second reading, it was so mauled in committee that the Government dropped it. The measure and its vicissitudes reflected the impression made on all Parties by the General Strike. The crucial amendment from the Liberals, dealing with the definition of a general strike, was said to have been approved by the Cabinet.[18] As things turned out, the unions had to wait for another fifteen years, by which time not only did they have a Labour Government with a majority large enough to make easy the fulfilment of the Party's programme, but they had as perhaps its most powerful member a man who had been at the centre of the General Strike, Ernest Bevin.

The Act, however, was much more than an unpleasant reminder. It is doubtful if it in any real sense inhibited the unions so far as orthodox industrial action was concerned; but the Labour Party, too, had a compelling reason to be rid of it as quickly as possible, for it struck at its main source of funds; its income from affiliation fees was reduced by over one-quarter. Party supporters could, under the Act, continue to make a declaration of their willingness to pay a political levy instead of their willingness being taken for granted unless there were an individual declaration to the contrary. The fact remained that, partly at least because of the license given by the Act, the proportion of union members making payments to their unions' political funds fell very sharply after 1927. In the previous year, the figure was 77 per cent, in 1943 it was 42 per cent. It was stated that, while before the Act only 78,000 members of the thirty-two biggest unions withheld the political subscription, within one year of the Act the number not contributing rose to over one million, and by 1943 to well over three millions. In the interval, it should be noted, trade union membership had greatly increased — from 5,218,000 to a record total of over eight millions — but it is clear that the proportion of the membership subscribing was very far from keeping pace with this rise. The Agricultural Workers' Union is an extreme case; its membership rose between 1927 and 1945 from almost 30,000 to 110,000; the members subscribing to its political fund remained practically stationary. The Locomotive Engineers' and Firemen's Union may provide a better criterion; its membership in this period rose from 48,000 to 68,000, its political subscribers only from 19,000 to 23,000. When 'contracting out' was restored by the Act of 1945, the picture changed; the percentage of trade union members liable to political contributions rose in

two years from 45 to 91. The amount of affiliation fees due to
the Party shot up from about £52,000 in 1945, to nearly
£81,000 in 1947, and £130,000 in 1948.[19]

The trade union leaders, no doubt chastened by experience,
addressed themselves, not very vigorously, to a policy of re-
trenchment. There was still the need for trade union organisation and doctrine to be strengthened and adjusted to new economic circumstances. In his address to the T.U.C. in 1926, the
President had demanded a 'new conception of the use and purpose of this Congress as an Industrial Parliament of Labour',
to evolve a programme for 'economic democracy', and had
even ventured to suggest that 'a scientific wage policy for the
unions required to be thought out', centred on a basic wage
'correlated to the index of industrial production'. In 1927, the
General Council's Report returned to the theme of a more
effective central government for the movement, and asked for
a greater measure of co-ordination of 'general basic principles'
through the medium of the General Council. In that year, too,
the Council reported on its remit of 1924, to examine a resolution that the number of trade unions should be reduced to an
absolute minimum and that, for this purpose, the aim should be
so far as possible organisation by industry, instead of the existing medley of unions of various sorts, with ill-defined spheres of
influence and conflicting policies. The Council's conclusion
was, however, that a scheme of organisation by industry would
be impracticable, and that voluntary co-operation or amalgamation was the only alternative.[20]

In fact, the policy of centralisation and consolidation, while
as a theory attractive, was in large measure stultified by the
separatism of the T.U.C.'s members. The smaller ones were
reluctant to give up their identity and their ambitions of becoming larger. The powerful general unions, by accepting the
thesis of organisation by industry, would have condemned the
conception on which they were based, since they straddled a
variety of industries. All were unwilling to give up their autonomy so far as their own particular policies were concerned.

In this they were little different from employers' associations. The latter certainly were better organised as units, and their spheres of operation more clearly prescribed. There was much less likelihood with them of demarcation disputes, although these were not entirely lacking. But when the General Council of the T.U.C. held up the National Confederation of Employers' Organisations, later to become the British Employers' Confederation, as an example of the kind of central co-ordination it wished to achieve, and used it as a bogey for its own constituents, it was, whether knowingly or not, exaggerating the Confederation's authority. The members of the Confederation, like those of the T.U.C., were opposed to any surrender of control over their own affairs, and where they presented a united front, it was generally on very broad issues, such as labour or Government encroachment on the functions of management. As in the T.U.C., it was the large associations that decided policy even in this narrow field.

Dominating the industrial scene, partly by reason of the personalities of the leaders, partly because of their sheer size and strategic position, were the unions or federations of miners, engineers, transport workers, and the mass of 'general' workers. Large sections of the last two groups had come together to form, in 1921, the Transport and General Workers' Union, from an amalgamation of the majority of the unions affiliated to the Transport Workers' Federation. There was no limit to its province, and under the dynamic leadership of Ernest Bevin it grew enormously. To the eighteen unions which formed it in 1921 were added no fewer than twenty-nine more by 1939, covering a huge aggregation of workers in a variety of occupations, of whom perhaps one-half were transport workers. Its only rival in this genre was the equally catholic National Union of General and Municipal Workers, which was built on the foundations of the old Gasworkers' Union; perhaps a quarter of its membership was in municipal undertakings.[21]

During this period, the trade unions in general, and the T.U.C. in particular, reverted to a more conciliatory and constructive approach to labour problems, reminiscent in its fundamentals of the 'New Model' attitude. Many factors entered into this. The General Strike had been a disillusioning experience; if the trade unions were to resume their forward march, a re-orientation of outlook was a sheer necessity. Funds suffered a catastrophic fall, and membership declined sharply, until by 1933 it was almost back to the pre-war total of 4 millions, compared with its 1920 peak of 8 millions. Private enterprise might have its faults, but the economy of Britain was built around it, and it seemed a matter of self-preservation to reinforce it, at least until the economic situation improved. This was no time for doctrinaire experiments. The Labour Party in office found itself incapable of producing panaceas for the country's plight, even if it had had the power to get them through Parliament. The trade unions had to do the best they could for themselves in their own way, and this way was to find common ground with the employers. Militancy became a luxury for extremists, whose motives were suspect both to the leaders of many trade unions and to the Labour Party. The National Union of General and Municipal Workers took a lead, which others followed, in barring Communists from holding union office, and the policy was later espoused by the T.U.C. itself. Ernest Bevin could now proclaim open distrust of Russia, in holding that Russian trade was '10 per cent orders and 90 per cent propaganda', and in denouncing Russian imperialism.[22]

Let business by all means be big; let it become even bigger; but let the trade unions match it in size and power, and let them insist on a working partnership. To acquire and justify this status, the trade unions must acquaint themselves with the needs and techniques of management, and must play their part in the reconstruction of industry on a sounder and more efficient basis. There must be greater productivity, and the workers must share in its rewards.

The T.U.C., which now had a General Secretary, Walter Citrine, himself a notable exponent of these ideas, became the platform of the new gospel. Encouraged by its attitude, and inspired by the need for employers and workers to pull together in their own interests, Sir Alfred Mond, of Imperial Chemical Industries, in 1928 invited a Conference on Industrial Reorganisation and Industrial Relations, in which he and the Chairman of the T.U.C., Ben Turner, led strong contingents from both sides of industry. Among the representatives were men of the calibre of Ernest Bevin, J. H. Thomas, Citrine, Samuel Courtauld, Lord Ashfield and Lord Weir. Its recommendations were moderate and sensible. They aimed at improving and supplementing the existing machinery, and to this end advocated the establishment of a National Industrial Council, representative of both sides of industry. It was to be a sort of industrial parliament, which was to work out economic policies and advise the Government accordingly. The collaboration between the two sides would be reflected in the conduct of industry, and not least in industrial relations. Thus the Council should, through a standing Committee, make available as need be a Joint Conciliation Board to deal with any dispute which had proved impossible of settlement through the machinery of the industry concerned. There was to be no lock-out or strike pending the issue of the Conciliation Board's report. It was hoped that in this way all disputes would be resolved without stoppages, and without recourse to Governmental agencies. This would have been the logical development of the principle long recognised, that industry should have the right and responsibility to reconcile its differences without let or hindrance, and that trade unions of workers and employers should be accorded great powers for this purpose, and for the good governance of industry in general. There were, however, strong elements on both sides of industry which did not acknowledge the right of the parties to the Conference to speak on their behalf, and which still looked wryly at the rapprochement which it seemed to signify. While the T.U.C. officially supported the discussions and the proposals which emerged, the Federation of British Industries and the National Confederation of Employers' Organisations remained suspicious of joint action in the economic field. The Depression killed the scheme; yet the fact that powerful interests on both sides had come together to discuss large industrial issues, and had established a measure of common ground, was an indication of the trend towards a healthier industrial relationship and a hopeful augury for the future.[23]

The career of Ernest Bevin reflects fairly accurately the changes in the policy of the trade union movement after the First World War, partly, of course, because more than any other man he influenced that policy. The War had established him as an outstanding figure, conscious of the power he wielded, and determined to exploit it for labour's benefit. At the end of the war he tried to enter Parliament, on a programme of 'social revolution brought about by a freely elected Parliament', but was defeated. He then addressed himself to building up trade union strength, which he was prepared to use against the Government if need be, as when he acted as spokesman of the delegation which, in 1920, demanded that Britain should not help Poland against Russia. In 1921 he fused eighteen unions into the Transport and General Workers' Union, and turned to the project of creating an alliance with the miners and engineers, which would be invincible. He identified himself with, and planned the organisation of, the General Strike, his arch-opponent being Winston Churchill. With the General Secretary, Citrine, he afterwards persuaded the T.U.C. that the trade union movement should neither seek to overthrow capitalism, nor conduct a guerilla war against employers to extort piecemeal concessions, but that it should instead demand a voice in making industry more prosperous. The Mond–Turner talks he defended on the grounds that industrial problems were best dealt with by the leaders of industry, not by politicians. He was often impatient of the ineffectiveness of politicians, including those of the Labour Party (which he called the 'other wing' of the trade union movement), although he appreciated, none better, that his ideals could be fulfilled only by a partnership of employers, trade unions and the State; but the State should merely implement the plans produced by joint consultation in industry. 'Parliament,' he said, 'will never lead the industrial system. Parliament will follow the industrial system.' The way to run industry was by joint control of employers and workers, with the blessing of the State.[24]

As there was no limit to the scope of his own Union, so there was no limit to the province of the trade union movement. He advocated at different times the nationalisation of British industry, a United States of Europe, an Empire bloc, the international control of raw materials. He may indeed have let such large preoccupations interfere with the running of the largest and loosest union in the country. An official London bus-strike in 1937 was a failure, which caused bitter dissension in the union ranks. There were other indications that, while with vast energy, acumen and foresight he had created a great organisation, he had perhaps given too little time to making it efficient. What was beyond doubt, however, was that he and his trade union colleagues had, in their own way, and in an atmosphere far from favourable, given the trade union movement greater solidarity and an established place in the nation. Trade union views were listened to, if not always accepted, not only on labour matters, but on almost every aspect of national and even international affairs. As re-armament gathered force, and the Depression ebbed, the leaders became more confident and more assertive. If the opportunity came for labour again to mobilise its strength, hitherto partially obscured by economic circumstances, the trade union movement would be well situated to take full advantage of it.

REFERENCES

1. *Trade Union Documents, op. cit.*, p. 72;
   C. L. Mowat: *Britain Between the Wars* (Methuen, 1955), pp. 17–21.
2. *Trade Union Documents*, pp. 74–5.
3. K. G. J. C. Knowles: *op. cit.*, pp. 50–4.
4. B. C. Roberts: *The Trades Union Congress, 1868–1921*, pp. 345–8;
   C. L. Mowat: *op. cit.*, pp. 30–43.

5. B. C. ROBERTS: pp. 342–4.
6. *20th Abstract of Labour Statistics*, pp. 144–6;
   Survey of Industrial Relations, pp. 335–6;
   J. SYMONS: *The General Strike*, pp. 24–5;
   C. L. MOWAT: pp. 119–25.
7. D. H. ROBERTSON: 'A Narrative of the Coal Strike' (*Economic Journal*, 36 (1926), pp. 375–93.
8. *Trade Union Documents*, pp. 355–6.
9. D. H. ROBERTSON: *op. cit.*
10. *Ibid.*;
    J. SYMONS: p. 29.
11. *T.U.C. General Council's Report to Conference* (1926);
    T.U.C.'s Reports on National Strike (1927);
    Strike Fortnight (*Daily News*);
    Trade Union Documents, pp. 334–50;
    C. L. MOWAT: pp. 298–310.
    THOMAS JONES: *Whitehall Diary* (Oxford University Press, 1969), Vol. II, 1.
12. HEDGES and WINTERBOTTOM: pp. 158–60.
13. *T.U.C.'s Report on National Strike* (*op. cit.*).
14. J. SYMONS: p. 133.
15. GARDINER and ASQUITH: *op. cit.*, II, p. 363.
16. J. SYMONS: p. 226;
    F. WILLIAMS: *Magnificent Journey*, p. 398.
17. HEDGES and WINTERBOTTOM: pp. 118, 160–6.
18. C. L. MOWAT: p. 365.
19. House of Commons Debates, 12.2.46 and 3.2.49;
    B. C. ROBERTS: *Trade Union Government and Administration in Great Britain*, pp. 369–72;
    K. G. J. C. KNOWLES: pp. 97–8.
20. *Trade Union Documents*, pp. 75–6.
21. N. BAROU: *British Trade Unions* (Gollancz, 1947), pp. 22, 51.
22. A. HUTT: *op. cit.*, pp. 117, 124, 133.
23. *Trade Union Documents*, pp. 257–60.
24. TREVOR EVANS: *Bevin*, pp. 72, 137, 140.
    ALAN BULLOCK: *The Life and Times of Ernest Bevin*, Vol. I, pp. 316–45.

CHAPTER IX

TRADE UNIONS IN THE SECOND WORLD WAR

In the Second World War there was no excuse, as there had been in the first, for a make-shift labour policy. Not only was the experience of the first War available, but there was now in existence, as part of its legacy, a Government department specially designed to deal with labour matters. There was not even the excuse that the issues likely to arise in war had been neglected during the peace. On the contrary, a great deal of study had been devoted to them by experts, in anticipation of another war. It was recognised in the earlier discussions that the labour expedients of the first War had been in the form of negative restraints rather than positive compulsions, and that next time the latter must be adopted. As far back as 1927 the Ministry of Labour proposed that, in the event of war, along with the control of prices and profits should go the regulation of wage-rates by a Central Arbitration Tribunal. This idea was accepted by the Committee of Imperial Defence, as was a policy of conscription for industry as well as for the Services. As memories of the War faded, industrial stagnation settled down, breeding dullness and defeatism in Government departments as elsewhere.

The Ministry of Labour suffered from the general infection. It lost its earlier boldness, and became more and more obsessed with the need to do nothing which would disturb good relations between employers and workers. It inveighed against the principle of compulsion in regard to wages, labour mobilisation or the prevention of strikes, on the grounds that labour would not tolerate it even in the exigencies of war. Thus the idea was gradually abandoned, and when war did come, in 1939, there was little to show, even in blue-prints, for the long deliberations

of the planners in this field. There was a revised version of the
Schedule of Protected Occupations, devised in 1917. There
was the draft of a Control of Employment Bill, and even this
diffident measure was emasculated as a result of labour protests
in and out of Parliament. In short, labour policies at the outset
of hostilities were far less comprehensive and forceful than those
hurriedly extemporised in the first War.[1]

There was one improvement: the Ministry of Labour became, with some reluctance on its part, the Ministry of Labour
and National Service. There was thus one agency, instead of
two as in the last war, to implement a total man-power policy,
if one should be declared by Government. Conscription for the
Services had already been introduced. From the start, therefore, there was at least an administrative machine to co-ordinate the needs of industry and the Forces. There was as yet no
indication that the new Ministry would take full advantage of
its authority. This state of comparative unpreparedness was of
course not due solely to the ultra-cautiousness of successive
Ministers of Labour. It was largely a reflection of the inadequacy of Government policy as a whole. So far as possible —
and much farther than practicable — it was to be a case of
'business as usual', with the Ministry confining itself to its normal peacetime functions in regard to industrial matters, and relying for support on the public-spiritedness and goodwill of
organised labour and employers. In particular, trade unions
and employers' organisations were to continue their traditional
rôles of determining the conditions of employment, and pre-
serving industrial harmony, with the Ministry's help if invoked.
It was forgotten that 'business as usual', as insisted on by both
employers and labour in the last War, 'had impeded the
mobilisation of war-making power, and cost the nation dear in
suffering and death'.[2]

The official approach was partly, too, the result of current
circumstances and attitudes. The political and industrial atmosphere was not conducive to whole-hearted effort, still less to
self-denial. The military stalemate in the 'phoney war' made

for a lack of urgency. There were still, in April, 1940, a million unemployed. The trade unions had for years been living in the shadow of mass unemployment, and were sceptical of the need for drastic controls. They were not well-disposed towards the National Government, which they blamed for the failure to deal effectively with the economic situation. They had acquired greater stature in the first War and, while they were solidly in support of the struggle against Nazism, they saw in it the opportunity to renew the advance of their power and policies which had been slowed down by the depression. Their leaders, like Walter Citrine and Ernest Bevin, made no secret of these aspirations. At the T.U.C. in 1939, Citrine declared that the trade union movement must emerge from the war with more power than ever before. Both trade unions and employers' associations had evolved into strong organisations, and were jealous of their authority. They would no longer be content, as in the last War, to be consulted by Government; they would insist on sharing with it the responsibility for policy-making in economic and social matters.[3]

Before the outbreak of war, the T.U.C. and the British Employers' Confederation had been consulted by the Minister of Labour with a view to giving their co-operation when the emergency materialised. There were bound to be in due course much the same difficulties as in the first War — shortages of workers, questions of dilution, the mobilisation of labour to meet war demands, and, above all, the need for industrial peace — as well as the difficulties which would arise from the vulnerability of the economy to air and sea warfare. Were there to be control of wages and compulsory arbitration in disputes? The Minister sounded the two bodies on such matters, but the response was not cordial. The T.U.C. gave qualified assurances of support for the Government, on condition that prices, profits and foodstuffs were controlled; wages, however, were to find their natural level. They refused to commit themselves to drastic regimentation. So far as the control of labour was concerned, they made startling and revealing proposals; this matter was to be

entrusted to national committees for the chief industries, which
would be given authority to deal with the use of labour. In
short, the Government was to vest executive powers in the representatives of industry. The Government, of course, rejected
this idea, and the discussions bogged down.[4]

The T.U.C. also seized the opportunity to ask the Prime
Minister, Neville Chamberlain, for amendment of the hated
Trade Disputes Act of 1927. They could hardly have been hopeful of a sympathetic response; it was suspected that he, and not
Winston Churchill, had been largely responsible for the Government's uncompromising attitude during the General Strike.
He refused to give any assurance to this effect, curtly stating
that any prospect of amendment would in effect be conditional
on the continued good behaviour of the trade unions. The principle that Government must always in its labour policies carry
with it the spokesman of industry, was, however, given immediate recognition, as the Ministry of Labour had planned, by the
establishment of the National Joint Advisory Council, representative of the T.U.C. and the British Employers' Confederation. A tentative approach to State interference was made with
the Control of Engagement Order, 1939, which 'belied its
name'; but there was no attempt to grapple with the realities
of the situation. These were for the time being disguised, for the
stagnant pool of unemployment was only gradually being
drained. Early on, however, an unscrupulous competition between employers for skilled labour developed. There was the
threat of a rising spiral in wages and prices, which first manifested itself in the coal-mining industry, and in which the
Government was perforce involved. There the owners made the
offer of a wage increase conditional on Government permission
to raise coal prices. The Government, fearful of a clash with the
Miners' Federation, agreed to this. As the tempo of the war-
effort speeded up, and certain classes of labour and goods became scarcer, wages and prices rose even faster than at the beginning of the first War. The economic advisers to the Government demanded a thorough-going policy of state-regulation of

I

wages through a national tribunal, coupled with restriction of profits. The Minister of Labour looked with misgivings at such proposals, or indeed anything which savoured of compulsion, and which would therefore be unpalatable to unions and employers. The Chancellor of the Exchequer warned the National Joint Advisory Council of the dangers of inflation, and was flatly told by the General Secretary of the T.U.C. that the workers would not accept any reduction in living standards, but that the trade union movement might encourage voluntary savings. The Government fell back on the policy of restraining the cost of living, and therefore, it was hoped, wage demands, by price regulation and the subsidising of foodstuffs. At this stage, the Government was much criticised for its apparent incapacity for vigorous action, in this as in other departments.[5]

The Chamberlain Government fell, and was succeeded by the Churchill Government. Labour was strongly represented. The Labour Party supplied two of the five members of the War Cabinet, and there were four more Labour Ministers. One appointment was particularly striking; the new Prime Minister promptly followed a Lloyd George precedent by appointing a leading trade union official, Ernest Bevin, General Secretary of the Transport and General Workers' Union, to Cabinet rank, as Minister of Labour and National Service.

Bevin had never been a professional politician, although he did not hesitate to join issue with politicians, of whatever party, over political matters. He took it for granted that his stay in Parliament would be temporary, and his successor in the Union was made only acting Secretary. A trade unionist of long and high standing, he had been highly critical of Government policy in the War and before, and, shortly before his appointment as Minister, had threatened to resist with all the strength of his powerful organisation any policy involving conscription of labour.[6] He had a great pride and trust in the industrial joint machinery which, as he often boasted, he had done much to create, and was resolved to use it to the full in his new capacity, although, with the prestige of his office and his commanding personality, he would certainly exert heavy pressure on such of his old associates as were slow to respond to his views. He was a shrewd bargainer, and knew well the temper of employers and labour.

He had not sought powers greater than his predecessor's and presumably did not anticipate any need for them. From the outset, however, he found the pressure of events and of opinion within the Government too strong for a policy of half-measures. Chamberlain, now Lord President of the Council, had been Director of National Service in the previous war, and had experienced the difficulties of reliance on the voluntary principle. It was he, not Bevin, who convinced the Cabinet that both workers and employers must be made subject to direct restraints.[7] So far as the latter were concerned, the method adopted was borrowed from the Lloyd George régime: firms on essential work were designated 'controlled establishments', and made subject to 100 per cent Excess Profits Tax. In regard to labour, Defence Regulation 58A was made in May, 1940, under the Emergency Powers (Defence) Act, permitting the making of Orders through which control of manpower could be exercised. The National Joint Advisory Council had agreed to the formation of a Joint Consultative Committee which the Minister could consult on the measures required.

There were two main issues to be settled, whether there should be a system of central wage-regulation, and whether there should be a ban on stoppages, with machinery for compulsory arbitration. Hitherto, suggestions to this effect had been coldly received. The new Minister asked the National Joint Advisory Council for 'a little less democracy and a little more trust', and put to the Joint Consultative Committee the idea — not his own — of a Central Arbitration Tribunal, which would periodically prescribe or recommend to the appropriate joint organisations national standards for wage-fixing, and the principle of compulsory arbitration. The union representatives were unanimous, though the employers were not, in rejecting the proposals. The Committee proposed instead a scheme of its own, which sought, not very successfully, to reconcile the demand for national control with the free working of voluntary institutions. It agreed that there should be no stoppages of work and that, in the event of a dispute not proving capable of settlement through the industrial machinery, it should be submitted to some form of arbitration. It recommended, too, as was natural from a body representing trade unions and employers' associations, that terms and conditions settled by these means should be binding throughout the occupations concerned. The proposals were given statutory force in Order No. 1305, the Conditions of Employment and National Arbitration Order, July, 1940.[8]

The National Arbitration Tribunal, which was a part of the new machinery, suffered from the defects of the former Committee on Production. Indeed, its influence on national wage movements was rather less, if only because in the interval not only had much of industry evolved negotiating machinery of its own, but there now existed the Industrial Court. The Tribunal was not given any criteria by which to judge disputes from the national standpoint, nor was there any discernible pattern in its pronouncements. Either party to a dispute could appeal to the Minister — under the Industrial Courts Act, arbitration required the assent of both parties — who was required to refer the matter to the appropriate collective machinery, if any, and, failing settlement there within twenty-one days, to the Tribunal, or, if the parties wished, another form of arbitration, such as the Industrial Court. In either case, the award was binding.

The Tribunal in fact proved a useful supplement to the established methods, which was presumably all that the Minister and the Joint Consultative Committee wanted it to be.[9] Probably the greatest virtue of the Order was its moral effect: its prohibition of stoppages and the sanction of compulsory arbitration, which stimulated the parties to a dispute to exert every effort to make their own settlements.

There were other and more cogent reasons for the comparative peacefulness of industry. The country was better prepared than in the first War for war-time stringencies, and the regimentation which Lloyd George and his colleagues naturally shrank from was accepted with little question. The allocation of the population as between essential work and the Services was from the start recognised to be the responsibility of the State, not of the individual. As in the first War, the liability to military service was a deterrent to industrial discontent, and was on occasion deliberately employed as such, as in the engineering apprentices' strike of 1941. It is true that there was much greater emphasis in this war on industry, for there was much greater reliance than in the first on its products for waging war. On the other hand, the organisation of workers and employers was much more advanced, and the mechanics of joint consultation much more efficient. There was, in fact, less need for outside interference, as the Joint Consultative Committee held, although more than the Committee was prepared to admit. There was, too, much less political agitation. The three principal Parties — and, after the entry of Russia into the war, the Communist Party — were agreed on the active prosecution of the war. Thus, although a shop-stewards' movement made itself felt on the Clyde in 1939, and there was in 1940 a so-called National Shop Stewards' Council, with a strong Communist element, it lost, with the advent of the Russian alliance, the political bitterness which had characterised its prototype and was more of a nuisance to the trade unions than to the Government. The official trade union leadership was again vulnerable, because of its identification with Government controls. Its representatives were on a host of official bodies, including the National Joint Advisory Council and the Joint Consultative Committee, and the Central Production Advisory Committee which was set up soon after Bevin's appointment, and which became in 1942 the National Production Advisory Council, as well as on other consultative bodies. They were on the Regional Boards for industry, established in 1941, and on the local joint Production Committees. In short, there was hardly a facet of the war effort with which the unions were not directly associated.

Although strikes were more numerous than in the first War, they were also much shorter, and the average annual loss of working-days was under two millions, as compared with over four millions in the first War. The basic causes of trouble were much the same in both cases: over-long hours, frustration and loss of faith in trade union officials, because of their association with official policies of restraint. As in the first War, when strikes on a large scale occurred, the statutory sanctions against them were comparatively ineffective, and were indeed rarely invoked. (There were 109 cases of prosecution, involving 6281 workers, between 1940 and the end of the War.) This was well illustrated by the Betteshanger Colliery strike in 1942, when fines were imposed on a large number of men but were simply not paid in the vast majority of cases. When, in 1944, on the eve of the Normandy landings, there was a serious outbreak in the mining industry (which had given much trouble throughout the War — coal-mining accounted for half the total time lost by strikes in 1943, two-thirds in 1944, and one-quarter in 1945) involving about a quarter of a million men, the experience of the first War was repeated; mass defiance, when the country was in straits, forced the Government to renounce legal prosecutions, and to make substantial concessions to the strikers.

The Minister of Labour, unwilling to concede that the continual flare-ups could be the result of internal combustion, arranged in 1944 for severe measures directed against political agitators. Defence Regulation IAA made it an indictable offence to 'instigate or incite' stoppages in essential industries. Defence Regulation IA was even amended to proscribe peaceful picketing if it was calculated to interfere with essential services. Although these fresh regulations aroused a good deal of resentment in both trade union and political labour circles, they were essentially cautionary, and were never, in fact, used. It is to be doubted if they were due to any real apprehension on the Minister's part of a serious threat to the national effort; rather they were prompted by resentment of disruptive tactics directed against the official trade union leadership.[10]

The idea of central wage regulation was never seriously pursued. The menace of inflation, with wages and prices chasing each other, was early recognised, but the hostility of the Ministry of Labour to any open restraints on wages, as likely to produce unrest, acquired new strength with the arrival of Bevin. While still General Secretary of his Union, he had curtly repudiated the economists' views in this matter, and he was going to do nothing now to weaken the unions' bargaining position, rather the reverse.

The Government realised that the example of the coal-mining industry, in its overtly making a wage-increase conditional on a corresponding price-increase, was too crude to accept as a precedent. It had, in effect, to give way, under somewhat similar circumstances, in the case of agriculture, where, under pressure from the Minister of Agriculture, supported by the Minister of Labour, a subsidy was given to farmers which would meet — and more than meet — increased costs, including a wage-advance. This proved to be a signal for a series of wage-claims in other industries. The policy of stabilising prices, through subsidies and price-controls, was adopted in 1941 as the answer to the producers, without the corollary of proportionately higher direct costs to the consumer, and was hailed as the ideal deterrent to higher cost of living and accompanying wage-increases. The policy was extended beyond essential supplies to essential services, including shipping and transport, with ingenious variations on the same theme.

It was hoped that such measures, and a public awareness of the need for self-control, would be sufficient. The Government did indeed appeal to the public conscience, through a White Paper, but this was almost contemptuously received by the T.U.C., in draft, and so watered down in deference to it, to obviate any suggestion of wage-control, that it had little effect. Earnings had risen by nearly one-third in less than twelve months from the outbreak of war. By July, 1941, the Minister of Labour had to admit that, while the cost of living had risen by 28 per cent, earnings had gone up 43 per cent. He justified this on the grounds that the higher earnings were the reward of longer hours and greater effort, and that wage-rates had advanced only 18 per cent. The argument was not entirely sound; the extension of piece-working, which the Minister did his best to encourage, was often done in a haphazard way, and not infrequently was merely a method of paying more in an effort to maintain something like the old standard of output.

The critics were not satisfied, and the weakness of the Minister's case became more apparent as the shortage of labour, especially unskilled labour, became more acute. A year or so later he could no longer assert that wage-rates were lagging behind the cost of living; they had caught up, and were now well in front. In 1944, the Chancellor of the Exchequer, Sir John Anderson, revealed that, whereas in 1941 wage-rates were 21 to 22 per cent above the 1939 level, in 1943 the increase was 35 to 36 per cent, and that 'during the period over which the cost of living was rigidly stabilised, wage-rates rose by about 15 per cent'.[11]

Between 1940 and 1944 the amount of Government subsidies rose from £72 million to £215 million. Wage-rates, which in 1940 had risen 6 per cent less than the cost of living, had in 1944 risen 11 per cent more. Over the War period, the cost of living (as then assessed, on a somewhat elementary basis) rose by one-third, wage-rates by one-half, and earnings by four-fifths. Whatever the justification for this disparity, it certainly could not be claimed that the Government's expensive policy had achieved its aim to stabilise wages.[12]

A much stricter control was exercised over the movement of labour, and here the influence of Ernest Bevin was marked. He did not relish the principle of compulsion in this any more than in other labour spheres; but there was really no choice. There had been much criticism in Parliament and the press of his apparent failure to mobilise the resources of labour, and this no doubt helped to force unpleasant decisions, and to prepare the public for them. The principle of direction of labour was certainly not Bevin's idea; but the conditions in which it worked clearly owed a great deal to him.

The main device was the Essential Work (General Provisions) Order, of March, 1941, with subsequent variants to suit the circumstances of certain special industries. Under these, the workers in 'scheduled' undertakings within the prescribed industry were not permitted to leave their employment, nor could they be dismissed (except for misconduct), save with the consent of one of the Ministry's National Service Officers. Workers could be directed to work in scheduled occupations. There were, however, very important qualifications. Before scheduling was confirmed, the Minister of Labour must be satisfied that the terms and conditions of employment were not less favourable than those recognised in the industry, and that welfare provisions were adequate. Among the terms of employment must be a guaranteed weekly wage, payable even if work were temporarily not available.

Such safeguards were only reasonable where labour was to be 'frozen' or directed; but they represented a tremendous advance in status and security for a vast number of workers, including many in those less protected occupations from which the Minister's own Union drew most of its strength. Thus it must have given him peculiar satisfaction to contrive and impose in 1941 a system of decasualisation for the docks industry, where he had been known since 1920 as 'the Dockers' K.C.' It was significant that in the Docks Scheme, Bevin realised his ideal of control shared equally between workers and employers, with the State acting as a benevolent third party.

The Essential Work Orders made a great contribution to the smooth running of industry. They also gave a wonderful opportunity to the trade unions concerned to secure valuable concessions from the employers, concessions which in normal circumstances would have taken years to achieve. Employers were generally willing and able to pay the price in return for an assured labour supply and, if they were reluctant, the Government Departments concerned could and did apply pressure.

The Orders represented a remarkable success in reconciling labour aspirations with the national need. They were, of course, temporary, but the Minister well realised that the unions, if they were worth their salt, would not easily abandon in peacetime what they had gained, in particular the guaranteed wage and welfare facilities. The actual rates of wages could safely be left to them to deal with through the negotiating machinery, especially having regard to their increased bargaining strength.

The Essential Work Orders, since they required 'recognised' conditions of employment, gave a great impetus to the establishment of voluntary negotiating machinery. Altogether fifty-six Joint Industrial Councils of one sort or another were established or re-established between 1939 and 1946.[13]

There still remained industries where organisation on orthodox lines was not practicable, and where, therefore, the State must take the initiative. There were already Trade Boards, but their scope was limited; for instance, they were not authorised to deal with guaranteed wages. Bevin accordingly sought to establish statutory wage boards in industries where voluntary machinery was lacking or defective which could continue into peacetime, and which would extend and improve on the work of the Trade Boards. A model lay to his hand, in the shape of the Road Haulage Wages Board, set up under the Road Haulage Wages Act, 1938, in the promotion of which he had, as a trade union leader, played a considerable part. Towards the end of 1940, at his instigation, a joint council had been established for the distributive trades, and in 1943 he sponsored the Catering Wages Act, setting up the Catering Wages Commission and Wages Boards to fix wages and conditions in the catering trades. As in Road Haulage and in the Docks, the administrative agencies were tripartite, representing (though not officially) both sides of industry, as well as the State. They made recommendations to the Minister, who could promulgate them in the form of Orders.

The system was condemned by critics as 'parallel to Fascist control of industry by industrial corporations'. The critics came from both employers and trade unions, who feared the intrusion of the State into such matters as wage-determination.

Those apprehensions found expression when in 1944 the Minister carried the policy a stage further. He then presented to the Joint Consultative Committee his conception of statutory boards or wages councils, to replace trade boards, and with power reserved to the Minister to substitute them for voluntary joint industrial councils where these were not functioning satisfactorily. The Minister also harked back to an old idea, that agreements made voluntarily between employers and unions might be given legal force if both parties so desired. Both sides of the Committee saw in this a dangerous enlargement of State interference which would weaken the existing joint machinery. The T.U.C. too, were 'at first apprehensive lest a wide extension of statutory wages enforcement might retard the growth of the trade unions'. The Minister modified his scheme, but the Wages Council Act of 1945 was still a triumph for his views. It converted Trade Boards, and the Road Haulage Wages Board, into Wages Councils. It provided for the establishment of new Wages Councils, on the initiative of the Minister of Labour or on the application of the appropriate joint industrial council; but in either event the decisive consideration would be the absence or inadequacy of voluntary machinery. The Councils would be representative of employers, labour and the State, while the staff would be appointed by the Minister. They would make recommendations to the Minister on a wider range of matters than was permitted to the Trade Boards they replaced, including guaranteed wages, and the Minister, if he accepted the recommendations, would promote Orders in Parliament to give them effect.[14]

It was a logical enough development. The Trade Boards had been started in order to eradicate sweated labour in selected industries. The system had subsequently, in 1918, been extended, as recommended by the Whitley Committee, so as to provide for the establishment of Trade Boards in any trade where the lack of adequate machinery for wage-fixing made such provision necessary. The scope of Trade Boards had been severely restricted, to minimum wage-rates. With the Wages Councils Acts, there was instituted an elaborate negotiating machinery to cover all workers in any industry where voluntary machinery was lacking or inadequate, with power to make recommendations on a variety of topics, including holidays and the guaranteed week. Wages Councils might be regarded as a make-shift for orthodox joint industrial councils, but they might also be thought, by some, to be an improvement on the stock pattern. The State had a say in their deliberations, and the State gave the force of law to the decisions that resulted. The Trade Boards had been regarded with misgivings by some trade union leaders, on the grounds that their effect would be to discourage trade union organisation, since they would tend to be considered by the workers concerned to be really Government agencies. The decisive part played by the independent members would accentuate this impression. This view must have also influenced the unions' attitude to Wages Councils.[15]

The trade union movement, which had reached its peak membership in 1920, and fallen by 1933 to little more than half this height, began to recover as the Depression eased in the later 'thirties. In 1938 it had over six million members, and in 1943, over eight millions, its highest figure for the war period. The only outstanding development was the fusion in 1945 of the autonomous unions in the Miners' Federation into the National Union of Mineworkers. So far as the structure of trade unions as a whole was concerned, there was talk from time to time, as indeed there had been almost since the inception of the T.U.C., of the need for reorganisation, but nothing came of it. The trade unions were anticipating with confidence an extension in peacetime of their power and scope, and in 1943 Congress, 'having in mind the still wider functions and responsibilities of the Trade Union movement in the post-war period', instructed the General Council to examine trade union organisation. A thorough review was accordingly carried out, but the resulting recommendations were much more cautious than those emerging from a similar self-examination almost twenty years before. Then the need for a drastic reduction of the number of unions, on the basis of industrial unionism, had been categorically affirmed. In the interval, experience had proved that this policy ran counter to the policies of many of the T.U.C. members. The obstacles to industrial unionism had in fact become greater with the rise of the powerful general unions, and the General Council now merely advocated a higher degree of unity and co-ordination among unions serving the same industry, with if possible, federation as 'a loose form of industrial unionism'.[16]

The T.U.C. also addressed itself to the problem of the reconstruction of industry in the post-war period. It was obvious that the innovations of war, both in attitudes and organisation, must deeply influence the shape of things to come.

The Churchill Government had, almost as soon as it was formed in 1940, started to work out plans for a peace-time economy. Labour Ministers were closely associated with this work, and the first Minister to be set to the task was Arthur Greenwood. The unions' views were therefore sure to be taken into consideration at some stage of the deliberations, and they were of course directly interested in the programmes envisaged in the White Papers on Social Insurance and Employment Policy, issued in 1944. They had, however, special aspirations of their own, which even their political colleagues did not necessarily endorse to the full. Thus, while it was assumed that a Labour Government would nationalise certain industries, such as transport, there had been clashes in the past over the question of labour representation on the governing boards, in which the protagonists were Herbert Morrison and Bevin. The Transport and General Workers' Union had insisted that labour should be specially and directly represented, and that, in effect, the Minister responsible should be required to accept the nominations of the trade unions concerned. Morrison, on the other hand, maintained that vested interests, including unions, should have no part in the appointments, which should be solely on grounds of suitability and should be at the discretion of the Minister. The T.U.C. too, inclined to the latter view, but the deadlock continued, and repeated discussions between representatives of the Party and the T.U.C. failed to resolve it, until finally a compromise solution was arrived at.[17]

In 1944, there appeared the T.U.C.'s Interim Report on post-war construction. It proclaimed the need for Government to ensure full employment, but, with war-time labour controls in mind, and the threat to the independence of the unions inherent in the most benevolent State regulation, even under socialism, it insisted that the freedom of the unions 'to determine their own policy, and to pursue their normal activities', must not be interfered with. Prices must be controlled, but the T.U.C. would give no pledges as regards wage movements.

So far as union participation in the control of industry was concerned, the Report revived the idea mooted by the Mond–Turner Conference of a National Industrial Council, which would advise the Government on the formulation of economic policies, and be associated with their application. In those industries to be nationalised, there should be on the governing boards trade union nominees, who would be channelled through the T.U.C.; but on their appointment they would surrender their connections with the unions. The ultimate responsibility for such boards would rest with the Government, through the appropriate Minister. There should be Consultative Councils, on which the unions would be directly represented, but those bodies must keep clear of trade union functions. Private industries should be subject to supervision on the public behalf, through Industrial Boards, on which also the unions should be represented.

All this was a far cry from workers' control. No doubt the T.U.C. at the time was not optimistic about the prospect of an early Labour Government, and certainly it did not anticipate — nor was it alone in this — the struggle ahead to maintain the national solvency. Even allowing for this, however, it

was obvious that trade union doctrines had been much modified as a result of the sobering circumstances of the inter-war
years, and of the war itself.

It is, however, only fair to remember that extremism had not
been an ingrained characteristic of the trade union movement
since it achieved comparative respectability. By and large the
movement tended to be solidly, and even stolidly, conservative,
and policies involving social or industrial re-organisation were
appraised with one consideration always in mind — although
not necessarily paramount — namely their impact on the trade
unions themselves. That was one reason why for many years
socialism, as a political doctrine, was regarded, if not with open
disfavour, certainly with a great deal of scepticism. The trade
unions in their formative period, and especially under the
'new model' régime, had to a large extent come to terms with
capitalism. Before, and immediately after, the first War, the
syndicalists had indeed strongly influenced the thinking of the
leadership, but that influence expired with the collapse of the
General Strike. There was still a distrust of pure socialism,
which could after all mean the end of the trade unions; but between the Wars the trade unions and the Labour Party had
drawn closer together, largely because of the political and
economic vicissitudes of the period. This alliance did not imply
a complete identification of the interests of the two bodies; it
was an understanding, based on the assurance that the trade
unions would have a large, if not a decisive, say in the Labour
Party's programme. This alliance was, of course, much closer
than that of former days with the Liberal Party. The Liberal
Party had refused to become a 'workers'' party, and had indeed helped to build up the Labour Party, positively by electoral support in the first stages, and negatively by failing to give
labour an effective share in its organisation. The Labour Party,
in return for trade union support, was prepared to sacrifice some
of its independence of thought and action, and equally the
trade union leaders recognised that they must make concessions to the politicians' views, for the sake of having in

Parliament a party, perhaps even a Government, whose policies
they had helped to mould, and whose members they had helped
to elect.

REFERENCES

1. H. M. D. PARKER: *Manpower* (*op. cit.*), pp. 57, 424–5;
   W. K. HANCOCK and M. M. GOWING: 'British War Economy' (*History
   of the Second World War*, 1949), pp. 50–7, 60, 144.
2. HANCOCK and GOWING: p. 59.
3. H. M. D. PARKER: pp. 67, 78–9;
   P. M. INMAN: 'Labour in the Munitions Industries' (*History of the Second
   World War*, 1957), p. 374.
4. H. M. D. PARKER: p. 59.
5. *Ibid.*, pp. 60, 88;
   HANCOCK and GOWING: pp. 152, 164.
6. P. M. INMAN: p. 41.
7. H. M. D. PARKER: p. 94.
8. *Ibid.*, pp. 94, 425–6;
   P. M. INMAN: p. 317;
   N. BAROU: *op. cit.*, pp. 153–4.
9. Of 2559 cases reported under the Order up to the end of 1946, 1060
   were referred to the National Arbitration Tribunal.
10. H. M. D. PARKER: pp. 457–62, 470;
    P. M. INMAN: pp. 195, 393–4, 403.
11. H. M. D. PARKER: pp. 426–9, 433–4;
    HANCOCK and GOWING: p. 338;
    N. BAROU: p. 162.
12. HANCOCK and GOWING: p. 502;
    B. C. ROBERTS: 'National Wages Policy in War and Peace' (Allen &
    Unwin, 1958), pp. 28–33.
13. Ministry of Labour and National Service, *Report for the Years 1939–46*,
    p. 276.
14. H. M. D. PARKER: pp. 438–40.
15. K. G. J. C. KNOWLES: *op. cit.*, pp. 92–3.
16. N. BAROU: pp. 206–10.
17. G. D. H. COLE: *A History of the Labour Party from 1914* (Routledge &
    Kegan Paul, 1948), pp. 280–1, 290;
    E. L. WIGHAM: *Trade Unions* (Oxford University Press, 1956), pp. 131–3;
    R. KELF-COHEN: *Nationalisation in Britain* (Macmillan, 1958), pp. 196,
    228.

CHAPTER X

POST-WAR PROBLEMS AND POLICIES

THE post-war pattern of industrial relations was almost inevitable, in the light of the historical development of trade union organisation and policies, and of the trade union movement's relationship with politics and with Government. Like most British institutions, trade unionism had deep roots. The nature of the soil, and of the climate, might change, but the most that could be hoped for was that the plant would be able to adapt itself to conditions hitherto foreign to it.

There were certain prejudices and attitudes that had become ingrained in the movement. Its spokesmen had sedulously fostered the legend that it had survived and prospered in spite of unremitting persecution from Government, the courts, and the employer class. They had canonised the Tolpuddle martyrs as trade union pioneers who had suffered nobly in the cause, although in fact the incident had only a tenuous connection with, and even less significance for, the movement. The legend, like most legends, was only half-true. Once the nation entered on the path of reform, in the nineteenth century, with the gradual liberalisation of the constitution and of social and economic doctrine, the unions were given their share of the new freedom. They operated with increasingly little hindrance from Government, both by the tacit consent of the community at large, and by specific authority of statute. The trouble was that the more ambitious trade unions took on activities which were deemed to be ancillary to their basic functions and, more important, were outside the limitations which the statute law had from time to time laid down for their protection as well as for their restraint. As they expanded, their protective covering showed chinks, through which their opponents attacked them, as by resort to

K 137

what Sir William Harcourt called 'the rusty armoury of the common law'. Yet in their formative years, in the second half of the nineteenth century, there was no serious attempt on the part of Parliament to restrict their growth. On the contrary, as soon as legal weaknesses were exposed, Parliament was not slow to amend the law, until finally the law's restraints on trade unions as such were virtually abolished — all this within a period of under fifty years. The General Strike did produce a reaction. It was held by the Government that concerted attacks by trade unions might be designed to coerce the State, and that this must be prevented. It was also held that it was for the individual positively to declare his willingness to support the Labour Party through his union contributions, and not for the union to take his consent for granted. No doubt the Conservative Government responsible was willing to loosen, as the Trade Disputes Act of 1927 did, the bonds between the unions and the Labour Party; but the provision also represented a belated reversion to the doctrine of the freedom of the individual in such matters.

The allegation that the courts showed an inveterate hostility to trade unions was better substantiated. It was supported not only by trade union leaders but by politicians who had no particular affection for them. Thus Winston Churchill said in 1911, 'It is not good for trade unions that they should be brought in contact with the courts, and it is not good for the courts. The courts hold justly a high and, I think, unequalled prominence in the respect of the world in criminal cases, and in civil cases between man and man, no doubt, they deserve and command the respect and admiration of all classes in the community, but where class issues are involved, it is impossible to pretend that the courts command the same degree of general confidence. On the contrary, they do not, and a very large number of our population have been led to the opinion that they are, unconsciously no doubt, biassed. . . .' [1]

The evidence suggests, however, that, while the courts' decisions might be awkward, for political parties as well as trade unions, they were not deliberately directed against labour; rather were they an expression of the ancient and well-founded view of the judiciary that the growth of powerful corporations, of whatever sort, was a potential menace to the freedom of the subject, and that they should be closely controlled by law. In pursuit of this view, the courts tended on occasion, although by no means as a consistent policy, to interpret such laws as were relevant to trade unions in a way which may well have been the way the legislators had intended, as was argued in the Osborne case, but which took too little account of changing circumstances and public opinion. There is little or no proof that the courts were being deliberately retrogressive or vindictive, or that they of set purpose misinterpreted the law as it stood.

So far as employers were concerned, there had always been in their ranks strong, and frequently bitter antipathy to trade unionism. Trade unions were regarded by many employers as avowed enemies of their class, as destroyers of the direct relationship between the employer and his workers, and as a force designed to weaken the employers' bargaining power in regard to labour. This distrust persisted, and probably in the nature of things always would be a factor. Employers' associations were built up, whose primary function was to counter the unions. They were, at the same time, essential to the operation of trade unions, and were increasingly welcomed and even encouraged for this reason by the unions themselves.

On the other hand, it should be recognised that there always had been employers, and often powerful ones, who strongly favoured trade unions, and helped in their establishment, either because the effect of collective bargaining was to minimise competition by imposing a common set of working conditions, or because it was increasingly realised that they were necessary to the good government of industry, and to the effective functioning of the modern forms of private enterprise. The shrewder and more far-seeing employers, like their counterparts in the unions, had long appreciated that each was necessary to the other. Capitalism meant, among other things, employers bargaining with labour on a large scale, and for such collective bargaining, collective agencies were indispensable. On the other hand, the disappearance of capitalism would mean the end of the trade unions, in the sense in which they were originally conceived and were still regarded by the generality of their members.

There were factors in the trade union movement which gave it a certain direction and kept it within a fairly narrow channel. In spite of the legal, political, economic and social status it had acquired, greatly aided by the exigencies created by two wars for national survival, it held fast to its original inspiration, the negotiation of better wages and conditions on behalf of its membership. The trade unions might, and did, insist on rights and functions which might be thought secondary to this prime aim, and they might indeed exert such influence on the nation's activities in general that they could be called, as they were by Winston Churchill, a fourth estate of the realm. They remained, however, dedicated to their original purpose.

Despite the widening of their horizon, it might even be said that their interpretation of their *raison d'être* had become narrower as their strength grew. The craft unions of a hundred years before, which had laid the foundations of the trade union movement, had campaigned for better wages and conditions, but they had also taken it for granted, as a natural function, that they should seek always to enhance the status of their crafts, and had not hesitated to deal severely with employers or workers whose actions prejudiced this. They had sought to give security to their members, by preventing redundancy, by finding alternative work for their unemployed, and by making provision for sickness and old age. Not least, they had tried to instil a sense of responsibility in their members, and a better appreciation of their rights and privileges, through education.

This conception of trade union functions was bound to contract to a considerable extent as the State took more and more upon itself the responsibility for social services. By the outbreak of the First World War the 'welfare state' had taken shape, and all political parties were committed to its support. They were, indeed, committed to its further improvement, for with the widening of the franchise to include all classes, and with the resulting preponderance of the 'working class' in electoral affairs, the promise of ever more generous social benefits became almost a condition of political survival.

It was not only a matter of politicians seeking votes. The growth of socialism had a particular effect on trade union doctrine. Socialists believed that it was an obligation of the State to provide all social benefits, and that attempts on the part of trade unions to provide them out of their own funds, or even to make them a charge on industry, was to obscure and obstruct the true faith. Thus, for the unions to try to negotiate with employers supplementary pensions or safeguards against redundancy, was something to be deprecated.

All this had a two-fold effect. The trade unions were deprived of the main justification they had had for acting as benefit societies, and were forced to concentrate on a narrower field, or find new activities. Conversely, the workers lost much of their interest in the trade unions as benefit societies, and looked to State agencies to provide them with the social insurances they needed. They looked to the unions for one thing, to increase the value of their labour.

In this re-orientation of trade union policy, the pressure of forces outside the movement was reinforced by a quite independent development, a shifting of power within the movement. New giant unions had come on the scene, the 'general' unions, who both by reason of their size and because they drew their recruits from almost every kind and grade of industry, were bound to exert tremendous influence over the whole field of trade unionism. Their strength, however, continued to lie in the lower ranks, the labourers, on whose behalf they had first been formed. In so far as organisations so heterogeneous could have an over-all policy, it was one dictated by this large and vocal element. It was from this section that the leaders tended to come, partly because of this, and partly because the labourers' spokesmen had to be tough and aggressive, as well as shrewd, to gain and hold their positions. They had the qualities and the limitations of their background. They were liable to be profoundly contemptuous of theory, while the massiveness of their armies gave them a supreme and perhaps exaggerated confidence in their own strength.

There was one policy guaranteed to give satisfaction to all, and offence to none, and that was to use all the means to hand to force higher wages from the employers. The simplest formula was a flat-rate increase for all the grades concerned, and the measure of success achieved was made manifest in the marked narrowing of the gap between the wages of skilled and those of comparatively unskilled workers.[2]

The 'general' unions were jealous of any encroachment on their sprawling and rather precarious empires, whether from other unions — who, if they shared the same slice of territory, had the option of merging in the larger union — or from the T.U.C., or from politicians of whatever complexion, or from Government. No type of trade union had ever been more insistent on autonomy and independence. The size of the 'general' unions, and the personality of their leaders, and particularly of Ernest Bevin, had enabled them to exert a decisive influence on the policies of the whole trade union movement.

The movement's position in relation to politics was somewhat peculiar, and reference has already been made to its general character. Since the movement had officially thrown in its lot with the Labour Party, it had, through its own successful nominees for election, contributed a substantial proportion of the Party's Parliamentary strength. In 1918, out of 57 Labour M.P.s, 49, or 86 per cent, were sponsored by the unions, and, although the proportion inevitably declined as the Party made a wider electoral appeal, it remained very substantial. In 1945, when the Party was returned to power, out of 393 M.P.s, 120 were trade union nominees. When the Cabinet was formed, this fact was duly recognised, and out of a Cabinet of twenty members, nine had trade union connections.[3]

There was a sharp distinction to be made between trade union membership and the trade union movement as the ally of the Labour Party. Only a minority of the unions affiliated to the T.U.C. was affiliated to the Party, and, even within the unions that were affiliated, membership was by no means synonymous with membership of the Party. The Trade Disputes Act certainly prevented the almost automatic enrolment of political recruits which had operated previously; but the almost total failure of the Party to recruit supporters from the vast intake into the trade union movement in recent years could not be excused, even by Labour defenders, on this ground. While the membership of trade unions affiliated to the T.U.C. had been increased during the War by nearly two millions, thus restoring it to its pre-war peak, trade union affiliation to the Party showed little or no advance. In 1945 only about one-third of all trade unionists were affiliated to the Party; of the huge accession of trade union strength during the War, it was estimated that only about one in a hundred joined the Party.

This was in marked contrast to the experience of the first War. The decay of enthusiasm was particularly marked in the case of the general unions. In 1937, long after the Trade Disputes Act, over 70 per cent of the membership of the National Union of General and Municipal Workers was affiliated to the Party, while in 1946 the proportion was down to 30 per cent. In the Transport and General Workers' Union, there had been a fall from 57 per cent to 37 per cent.[4]

Nevertheless, whatever might be the political views of trade unionists, the constitution of the Labour Party rested on the well-founded assumption that the trade union movement was the partner — the senior partner — of the political labour movement. In the Party's Annual Conference, and in its National Executive, a dominant rôle was assured to the trade union representatives. As affiliated organisations, the unions were empowered to send to the former body one delegate for every 5000 members on whom affiliation fees were paid—which was not necessarily the total of members who paid the political levy — with one vote for every 1000 members. This meant in practice that the union delegates, working together, could control a large majority; indeed, the six largest unions, two of them general unions, as a bloc could alone exercise a decisive influence on the Conference's deliberations. This situation was even more marked in the policy-making National Executive, which was elected by the Conference. Of its 28 members, 12 were elected by the union delegates, and 6 by the Conference as a whole, so that the unions could, if they wished, ensure the appointment of a solid majority of their choice.

By far the greater part of the Party's finances was also derived from the trade unions, quite apart from the money spent by the latter in the constituencies on their favoured candidates. While the T.U.C. itself was not affiliated to the Party, it held exactly one-half the seats on the National Council of Labour, and was by this and other means closely consulted by the Party on its policies. The T.U.C. could therefore honestly proclaim, and frequently did, that the trade union movement had 'never subordinated itself to political parties, or taken its instructions from Governments', but the Labour Party could not claim a similar independence of the trade union movement.[5]

Apart from the obvious propriety of the T.U.C.'s attitude, too close an alignment with one party would have been potentially very dangerous. In the first place, there were still many in the trade union movement who, regardless of their political sympathies, disliked the idea of its becoming directly involved in politics; and there were politicians, on the left as well as on the right, who shared this view. There were many trade unionists who had no great interest in the Labour Party, or who positively opposed it, and it would have been foolish to alienate them. Even after the repeal of the Trade Disputes Act, which allowed unions to take it for granted that its members were adherents of the Labour Party unless they went out of their way to indicate the contrary, this was a serious consideration. In 1947, nearly 9 per cent of the membership of registered unions with political funds did not pay political contributions. Ten years later the proportion had risen to over 12 per cent or nearly one million members.[6]

Besides, the history of the movement demonstrated abundantly that a strong conservative streak ran through it, and in particular a distrust of left-wing doctrinaires. It was true that a section of the movement was still officially committed to the doctrine of a radical change in the ownership and organisation of industry; but leading elements had, for practical purposes, accepted the capitalist structure, and had based their own organisation and policy on the need to confront strong employers with strong trade unions, so as to wrest concessions, and ultimately a kind of partnership. It was simple enough for an industrial union, such as the miners' or the N.U.R., to take state-ownership as a slogan; it was more complicated in the case of such as the general unions, with a hold on every conceivable type of enterprise. In those very influential quarters a kind of schizophrenia had developed. The leaders had long preached the iniquity of the 'private' employers, and still did so to impress their more belligerent members; on the other hand, they had observed with approval the growth of employers' organisations, similar to their own, with which they could deal as equals. They would, indeed, have been lost without the employers — perhaps literally; for there was still a nagging uncertainty as to what precisely would be the functions of trade unions if the control of the means of production, distribution and exchange were indeed vested in the State. This was no doubt one reason why, in planning nationalisation — or more correctly, in postulating the principle of nationalisation, for there had been no real thought given to how it should be made to work — the unions as a whole had been willing to keep clear of the actual management of the new undertakings.

The danger of being identified with one political party became much more tangible when that party ceased to be merely a political pressure-group and achieved such strength as to be liable to provide the Government. In spite of all the precautions the trade union movement might take, in helping to shape the

Party's official programme, and in spite of the presence in Parliament of a solid trade union phalanx, complete domination of a Labour Administration would be impracticable. A Government could not long survive, in modern circumstances, if it appeared to be subservient to one vested interest, however strong. It was always possible that conditions might materialise to meet which the blue-prints worked out in advance might have to be drastically modified. It might be, although it was highly unlikely, that the political Labour leadership, when in power, would even override the views of the T.U.C. on important issues, as indeed had happened before the War. In that event, clearly the trade union movement must reserve the right to disown or challenge the Government's policy. Furthermore, there was the danger that, if the T.U.C. became the partner of a Labour Government, another Government might reasonably assume that it must treat the T.U.C. as in a sense part of the Opposition.

There was, of course, another element in the situation which would make any party reluctant to antagonise the trade union movement. A conflict might possibly precipitate widespread industrial unrest — only possibly, because the movement had become very chary of using its strength to put pressure on Government, except through the recognised political channels. Still, it was certain that industrial strife would be more likely to develop in an atmosphere of mutual hostility between Government and the movement. Further, a clash could become a political issue, in the sense that the movement could use it to rally its membership in support of the Opposition.

Finally, there was the question of the traditional relationship with one department of the Government, the Ministry of Labour. The Ministry was not simply an agency invested with special duties and powers as regards labour. Its civil servants might and would, with a high sense of responsibility to the community, produce policies devoid of political bias; but ultimately policy-making was vested in the Minister, who, in critical matters, would receive guidance from the Cabinet, and who must always be conscious of the electoral aspects of any labour matter with which he was concerned. A strong labour policy was not likely to emerge from this quarter.

At the end of the War, the trade unions were confronted with a combination of circumstances for which their past thinking had done little to prepare them. True, there had been blue-prints in anticipation of peace. In 1944, the Government had issued a White Paper on Employment Policy, which stressed the dangers of inflation, and the necessity for organised labour and employers to join with the Government in a common effort to withstand it, and in particular to ensure that a rise in the general level of wage-rates should be conditional on increased productivity. The T.U.C. for its own part had prepared its Interim Report on Reconstruction; but it envisaged a rôle for the trade unions which would be essentially the same as the old one, but would be more effective because economic and social policies in harmony with it would be in force.

For generations past, the trade unions had, with every justification, been obsessed with the problem of unemployment, and had come to accept it as endemic to the functioning of a capitalist society in peace-time. Their policies were all directed to one end: to prevent, at worst, the depreciation of organised labour, and, at best, to enhance its value, by an unremitting use of the trade unions' bargaining power. This policy had been to a certain extent modified in the national interest during the War, but by no means renounced. In any case (it was said) there would be no need for artificial compulsions on labour once the transition from war to peace was accomplished. There was talk of inflation; but trade union leaders had learned, in a harsh school, their own elementary, bread-and-butter brand of economics, which made them distrustful of new theories, and reluctant to accept new facts. And, after all, they asked, were the theories or the facts so new? As far back as the nineteenth century they had been threatened by the pundits with national catastrophe if they succeeded in their wage-demands. There would, no doubt, be a boom in the immediate post-war period, but experience had demonstrated beyond question that a slump would follow. The depression of the inter-war years had seared deep memories, which would be fresh in their minds for long years to come. Was Government to be trusted in matters affecting labour? It depended on the make-up of the particular Government. Were the trade unions, who had triumphed in the face of hostility from many quarters, now to hold their hand while all too transient economic forces were working in their favour; or were they to exploit them to the full in the sure anticipation of lean days ahead?

There was little doubt as to the answer, qualified though it might be. The Government should keep a strict watch on profits and prices, and take all measures necessary to maintain full employment short of labour controls. In the sphere of industrial relations, as indeed in all matters appertaining to labour, there must be a minimum of interference, since this was the province of the trade unions. There might be a case for the retention of compulsory arbitration in its present form, at least during the period of change-over from war to peace, which was bound to be a time of challenge to constituted authority; but this must be understood to be by grace of trade unions and employers.

Whatever Government were in office, it would surely do everything possible to avoid a clash with the unions, now at the peak of their power. With a Labour Government, the possibility of such a clash was indeed remote. There had been conflict on a previous occasion, but this time the Government was solidly entrenched, and clearly mandated to carry out prescriptions already agreed in principle with the trade union movement. A programme of nationalisation was duly put into effect, and assurances given that capital would now be harnessed without stint to social needs, including full employment.

It was certainly easy — too easy, said some — to make ample finance available. There was, in any event, no shortage of employment; on the contrary, the hunger for domestic goods and services, the continuing demand for armaments, and the paramount need to produce more and more for export, meant a

shortage of labour, despite demobilisation — or an excess of
employment, according to the point of view. Direction of labour
and the Essential Work Orders were abandoned as quickly as
possible, in deference to public opinion. There were official
regulations and priorities for materials and activities, but it was
a sisyphean task to control the laws of supply and demand. In
industries — and they were many — where the cost of higher
wages could fairly easily be passed on by the employers in prices,
there was an insatiable labour demand, and a correspondingly
low resistance to wage-claims. Industries not so fortunately
placed, but equally or more essential to the nation, remained
grievously under-manned. The atmosphere at first was one of
apathy, or at least acquiescence, which affected all parties, including the Government. Employers were being continually
adjured to make amicable wage-settlements for the sake of industrial peace, and the Ministry of Labour was always ready to
use its influence to this end, without much regard to economic
considerations.

It was not to be reasonably expected that, in such a climate,
the trade unions should voluntarily adopt a policy of self-denial,
and even more unlikely that, if they did, they could convince
their own membership. That inflation was rife, with prices
and wages blindly chasing each other, was only too apparent;
but even the professional politicians and economists were not
agreed on the remedy. There were some who doubted if there
was a disease at all, and indeed for those who could climb on the
roundabout, whether workers or employers, the game was
rather exhilarating. It was difficult enough to convince the
T.U.C., which represented the top leadership of the trade union
movement, that the unions had a direct responsibility, and that
it should accordingly endorse a policy which must be thoroughly
unpalatable to the mass of workers. For the T.U.C. to get its
constituent members to translate the policy into practice was
well-nigh impossible. It would be unfair, because of this, to
blame the T.U.C. for lethargy or irresponsibility; even if it had
had the will, it lacked the means to insist on an overall policy,

just as did its counterpart, the British Employers' Confederation.

Yet the task had to be faced. The Government was forced by events to realise that there might, after all, be an incompatibility between the unfettered working of the labour market and national solvency. The self-interest of a section of the community was no more synonymous with the interest of the whole than it had been in the nineteenth century; that it was a different and numerically larger section did not alter the fact. It was soon evident that positive action of some sort was essential if the country were to be saved from bankruptcy. A return to direction of labour on any appreciable scale was unthinkable. The Government might reverse its money policy, and adopt a course designed to reduce inflation. This would certainly check the alarming increase of personal incomes, but equally it would imply a contraction of employment and, on the latter ground alone, it would be stoutly resisted by the trade unions. The Government might impose wage-restraint, through some system of national control; that is, it could have a wages-policy. This was not likely, since as late as 1946 one of the most influential members of the Government, Ernest Bevin, had condemned this expedient on the score that it would weaken the trade unions. A little later, in 1947, the Labour Party did seriously entertain the idea; but it was anathema to most trade union leaders, notably Arthur Deakin, General Secretary of the Transport and General Workers' Union, who not only genuinely believed it to be impracticable, but also saw that under it their own strength would be curbed and diverted to serve the needs of the State.[7]

Any democratic Government would have vacillated in face of such a dilemma. Stern measures would, of course, have been unpopular in other quarters than labour. The Government was, however, by its nature peculiarly sensitive to trade union opinion; this had indeed been regarded as one of its particular qualifications for office at this time.

There remained only one resort, to accept the view that free collective bargaining was sacrosanct, and to try, by advice and moral pressure, to keep wage-settlements within bounds. Even this tentative approach was fraught with peril for the Government, for it could be construed as encroachment on territory traditionally reserved to trade unions and employers.

By 1946, the economic situation was menacing; costs, of which the wage element was a substantial part, were rising so fast as to threaten the stability of the whole economy, and, in particular, the expansion of exports, which was vital. It was imperative that the country should be warned of the perils inherent in present courses, and especially that influential part of it represented by employers and trade unions. The National Joint Advisory Council was duly consulted, and early in 1947 the Government issued a 'Statement on the Economic Considerations affecting relations between Employers and Workers'. It was a colourless production, which echoed the White Paper of 1944; 'every hint of resolution had been emasculated by the need to secure agreement from both sides of industry', and it was received with polite indifference.[8] A Government suggestion that labour should be drawn to the more unattractive industries of national importance by the offer of special inducements, was dropped on the insistence of Arthur Deakin and other union leaders; this would clearly be to interfere with the free play of collective bargaining. The Government then made a half-hearted attempt to achieve the same aim through a Control of Engagements Order (1947), but this was a timid measure, timidly used. An appeal by the Prime Minister for wage restraint evoked an immediate outcry from the trade unions.

The situation continued to deteriorate; import prices were rising; and in 1948, the Government took its courage in its hand, and, without the approval of the N.J.A.C., issued a more pointed warning in a White Paper on 'Personal Incomes, Costs and Prices'. It insisted that there was no justification for any general increase of individual incomes, and that rises in wages and salaries should be claimed or agreed only in exceptional cases; for example, to attract labour to essential under-manned industries. It agreed that Government intervention in wage determination would be 'an incursion ... into what hitherto had been regarded as a field of free contract between individuals and organisations', but added, significantly, that 'in order to avoid the undesirable necessity for any interference with the existing methods of free negotiation and contract', the Government would expect the parties to observe the basic principles outlined, and would itself adhere to them where it was directly concerned. (In practice, it failed to do so. When threatened in the following year and in 1951 with railway strikes in support of higher wages than the Railway Executive was prepared to concede, the Government showed none of the resolution it counselled in others. In the latter year it actually overruled the award of its own Court of Inquiry, to appease the unions. Nationalised industries, to say the least, did not set an example in withstanding the pressure for higher wages.)

However much they might condemn such unilateral pronouncements, the more thoughtful union leaders were impressed, and a majority of the T.U.C. was persuaded to support the cause of wage restraint, with certain important qualifications. This had an appreciable effect; there was a marked slowing down of wage-claims, and a stiffening of resistance to them, over the next eighteen months or more. In 1949, the real meaning of inflation, the disguised debasement of the coinage, was rudely and vividly brought home when the Government officially devalued the pound. At the same time, it urged the T.U.C. to continue and intensify the policy of wage restraint.

The General Council responded with remarkable courage, recommending that wage-claims should not be pressed unless the index of prices rose by over 5 per cent. True to the gospel of independence, it also rejected a Government offer to reciprocate by cushioning the policy of restraint with a statutory minimum wage. This had once been a trade union aim, but that was before the unions had become completely self-reliant. The General Council's recommendation was only narrowly endorsed by a special meeting of the T.U.C., and some of its champions were shortly to discover that they did not speak for their own members. Under the impact of devaluation and the Korean War, the merry-go-round of prices and wages resumed its giddy whirl. In 1950, the T.U.C. carried a resolution formally to end wage restraint, in defiance of the General Council's advice.

The T.U.C. had gone farther than its critics had believed possible — farther, perhaps, than the national employers' organisation would have gone if faced with a comparable task. Nevertheless, for all its good intentions, it had succeeded only in erecting a somewhat flimsy and leaky dam against a flow which it was powerless to arrest. It might be held that, unaided, it could not have succeeded, and that in any case to control the spate of rising wages was not the trade unions' business. On the other hand, it was a business in which they arrogated to themselves a major interest, and to that extent they must share the odium of failure.

The advent of a Conservative Government did not materially change the situation. The T.U.C. again declared that it was not concerned with politics, and it did not hesitate to issue further warnings against immoderate wage-claims. The Government was as reluctant as its predecessor to antagonise labour — in a sense, even more so, because it had to go out of its way to enlist the trade unions' goodwill, which the Labour Government had not. There was no move to implement the Conservatives' proposal, in their 'Industrial Charter' of 1947, to amend trade union law, as it had been left by the repeal of the 1927 Act, by replacing 'contracting out' by 'contracting in', and in other ways insisting on the voluntary nature of trade unions. This Government, too, appealed for wage restraint; and it, too, took the easy way out when confronted with wage-claims in nationalised industries. In 1953 it forced a settlement on the Transport Commission, and, in making a concession to the railway unions, set a standard for other wage settlements. An attempt by the Minister of Labour in 1952 to secure reconsideration of Wages Councils' awards, although strictly constitutional, had sent the General Council of the T.U.C. hot-foot to the Prime Minister to demand, and receive, assurances that there was no intention of interfering with the machinery of negotiation. The T.U.C. remained adamant against any suggestion, from whatever source, that there should be a national wages-policy, or even a national trade union policy in regard to wages.

The Government's attitude was, however, hardening. It had put its faith in a disinflationary money policy, which the trade unions, however much they disliked its manifestations, such as the reduction in subsidies, could not effectively resist. It was, however, anxious to supplement this means by others bearing more directly on the labour problem. The Control of Engagements Order had gone in 1950, and in 1952 there was introduced a Notification of Vacancies Order which, as its name implied, required employers to fill their vacancies through the Labour Exchanges. In 1954 the idea of an 'authoritative and impartial body', to consider the pattern of wage-claims in the context of the national economy, and 'to give advice and guidance as to broad policy and possible future action', was again put forward, this time by a Court of Inquiry into engineering and shipbuilding disputes, presided over by Lord Justice Morris. The Minister of Labour referred this proposal to the N.J.A.C., where it was received with scepticism, and a memorandum on the subject submitted by the Minister was suppressed in deference to the trade union side's objections.

Not only was the Government showing more determination at this stage — for example, in its publication in 1956 of a White Paper on the Economic Implications of Full Employment, issued without the backing of the T.U.C.; it seemed that, weary of recurrent crises, public opinion was becoming receptive of bolder proposals to deal with them. When, in 1957, another Court of Inquiry into disputes in the shipbuilding and engineering industries revived the proposal of Lord Justice Morris's Inquiry, the Government proceeded to adopt it. It set up a National Council on Prices, Productivity and Incomes. It also introduced a 'credit squeeze', with a Bank Rate of 7 per cent, and other checks on expenditure. These policies were heartily condemned by the trade union movement. So far as the new Council was concerned, neither its establishment nor its initial pronouncements were welcomed by the trade unions, which took the view that, being a Government-sponsored body, the Council must be prone to reflect Government opinions, which, as it happened at this time, the unions did not share. Its findings must therefore be suspect so far as they dealt with labour issues.

This attitude had a certain amount of justification, whatever the complexion of the particular Party in power. The Government, as representing the State, had become by far the largest of all employers of civilian labour, with around three millions of the working population under its control. It had a great staff of civil servants of one kind or another, whose number was generally increasing, and who, incidentally, were playing a very important part in the trade union movement. It had assumed the ownership of a considerable section of industry, through nationalisation, in railways, road, port and air transport, coal-mining, and electricity and gas supply. Although it might delegate its control to administrative bodies of its own appointment, it could not delegate its ultimate responsibility for the sound and efficient operation of the services concerned. It was associated with Wages Councils covering perhaps two million workers. It demanded that its own contractors should abide by the terms of collective agreements. It was therefore inevitable that Government should on critical occasions seek to exert an influence, whether openly or behind the scenes, on the course of wage negotiations. As has been seen, it had done so overtly several times to impose on the administrative agencies of nationalised industries a settlement more favourable to the unions than these agencies had thought desirable.

In 1955 Sir Walter Monckton, who as Minister of Labour had been associated with a policy of being ultra-conciliatory towards the unions, was replaced by Iain Macleod. In 1957 he went a good deal further than had his predecessor, in urging moderation on Wages Councils, by positively rejecting an agreement in regard to the wages of certain grades in the employment of the National Health Service. This was immediately assailed, with some plausibility, as an attack on the

negotiating machinery of industry, and a challenge to the trade
unions, who already, under the new leadership of the Transport
and General Workers' Union, had declared themselves im-
placably opposed to the Government's economic policy. Certainly the Government now seemed prepared to make a stand,
if it thought the ground were favourable, on a narrow front.
When the Transport and General Workers' Union endorsed a
strike of the London bus-workers in furtherance of a wage
demand, the London Transport Executive refused to give way,
and clearly had the Government's backing in doing so. It was
significant that, in spite of threats to spread the strike, it remained confined to the bus-workers, and the T.U.C., for one
reason or another, withheld active support.

It was noted, too, that the Ministry of Labour, which had
always been regarded as a peace-making body in industrial
relations, appeared on this occasion to make less effort than
usual to discover a face-saving compromise. The Ministry was,
after all, a department of the Government, and was bound to
have regard to Government policy. Suggestions were put forward that it was time for the whole machinery of arbitration to
be overhauled in the light of new conditions.[9]

The war-time Conditions of Employment and National
Arbitration Order had come up for review at the end of the war,
and the N.J.A.C. had agreed that it should be continued for the
time being. Officially the trade union movement did not favour
compulsory arbitration and, in the T.U.C.'s 1944 Report on
Post-War Reconstruction, it was linked with direction of labour
as undesirable and unnecessary. In practice, it had proved less
onerous than the unions had once supposed. The right to strike
was sacred; the exercise of the right was another matter. The
strike as a method of forcing a settlement had had its origin in
frustration arising from the inability to make progress with
claims, due to the refusal of employers to deal with the unions,
or to be reasonably forthcoming in negotiations. One result and
intention of the Order, however, had been to strengthen and in
effect extend the scope of collective bargaining, for it required

employers to observe terms and conditions agreed between the industry's representative organisations, regardless of whether or not they were members of those organisations. Some unions certainly found this a great convenience in securing settlements which were binding throughout their trade or profession, without their having first to build up their own organisation to the point where they could impose general standards by virtue of their bargaining power. If satisfaction could not be obtained through the normal processes of negotiation, then the issue could be remitted to a higher court, the National Arbitration Tribunal, or other appropriate body; and it was sometimes a relief to union leaders, as it was to employers' associations, to be able to tell their constituents that they had fought for their case as far as the law of the land permitted, and, if the settlement were unpopular, to attribute the blame to the Tribunal. The temptation to pass on responsibility was always inherent in any system of compulsory arbitration, and there were unions and employers who found the Tribunal a very convenient way to deal with their difficulties.

The union officials could always invoke the Order as precluding them from a course of action with which, in fact, most of them had little sympathy. Of course, the fact that they were debarred from calling strikes was exploited by unofficial leaders. The motives of the latter were various, but were often in one way or another highly personal; frustrated ambitions, dislike of officials, political prejudices, these and others were known to play a part in particular cases. It was not true that the Order prevented trade union militancy, as the demand for wage increases showed; but there was a tradition in certain ranks that militancy and strike action were one and the same. To men untutored in the techniques of bargaining, the strike was the simplest instrument of negotiation. To lead a strike, as the veterans of trade unionism well knew, was to ride a tiger, but this did not apply to men with no official responsibility. Lacking responsibility, they could resort to its use without premeditation and with little fear of retribution, and with the assurance of a cheap, if transient, popularity with their supporters.

If the trade unions had mixed feelings about compulsory arbitration, the employers were even less enamoured of the system. The most they could hope for from reference to the Tribunal or its equivalent was confirmation of their own proposals for settlement; it was almost unheard of for an arbitration court to give less than their final offer. Every employer, whether or not he was associated with collective agreements, was strictly bound to observe the awards, whereas, in the nature of things, his employees might, and not infrequently did, kick over the traces with impunity. The suggestion of a lock-out would invite dire consequences for the employer, but strikes in defiance of the law were common. Unofficial strikes were, from the employers' point of view, in some respects more awkward than official strikes. They were primarily a repudiation of trade union authority, and the employers could make little or no direct contribution to their settlement beyond lending a thankless support to the trade unions concerned. On the other hand, it was appreciated that to disown the Order might be to invite an outburst of industrial strife, although many employers were sceptical about this.

The truth was that whatever virtue was possessed by compulsory arbitration, it was not in the nature of a direct advantage to either employers or organised labour, although this might be an implication. Its real purpose was to preserve peace in industry, to protect the community from the disruption implicit in stoppages, by requiring both parties to disputes to settle their differences in an orderly manner.

Order 1305 was therefore continued, with the consent of both sides, on the understanding that either could at any time demand its review. It survived until 1951. Its revocation was ascribed by the Ministry of Labour to the headway made by that section of the trade union movement which was opposed to the prohibition of strikes, so that it finally 'became clear that the provisions of the Order which prevented strikes and lock-outs no longer commanded general assent'.[10] This was in fact a doubtful hypothesis. There was little evidence that the assent presumed to underlie the Order was any less general in 1951, when it was replaced, than it had been in earlier years. In 1945 nearly three million working days were lost in unofficial strikes, and this was a figure considerably lower than that of the previous year. It was an ominous fact that of the 1945 total, one-third was in the docks industry. In 1946 and 1947, the average annual loss ran at over two million working days, after which the amount declined, until 1950 showed the lowest figure for the post-war period so far, being well under one-and-a-half millions.

It was not an increase in the unpopularity of the Order that precipitated a crisis, but rather a recrudescence of unpopularity in a few hostile quarters, accompanied by a higher degree of publicity. The general unions had always been particularly sensitive in this matter. They had throughout their history prided themselves on their militancy, and there were powerful sections of their membership, notably in the docks industry, that refused to forgo a tradition in which they had been bred. The then General Secretary of the Transport and General Workers' Union, Arthur Deakin, therefore occupied a specially vulnerable position. He had become increasingly identified in the minds of his members with a policy of moderation, and the unofficial strikes in the docks industry were avowedly a challenge to his leadership. In 1950, there was a serious dock strike arising out of his Union's expulsion from membership of certain individuals, on the charge of being involved in unofficial activities. In the same year there was an unofficial strike of maintenance men in the gas industry, members of the other giant general union, the National Union of General and Municipal Workers. A strike of this nature might in any case be illegal under Section 4 of the Conspiracy and Protection of Property Act of 1875, but it was also a breach of Order 1305. Since it could not be ignored as a private quarrel, but was a matter of the public interest, the Government had little choice but to prosecute, which it did.

The General Council of the T.U.C. made it known that it

would press for an order ending the prohibition of strikes and lock-outs, but maintaining the obligations on employers as regards the observance of recognised terms and conditions, to which it attached much importance. In 1951, there was another dock strike, which attracted great attention. The Government again decided to prosecute — it was said, against the wishes of the Transport and General Workers' Union — and the case was heard by the Lord Chief Justice, with the Attorney-General leading for the Crown. It was, however, perhaps not so much the prosecution itself as the fact that the Crown failed to secure the verdict it sought, that created a furore. It was bad enough having strike leaders defying the law; it was intolerable to have the law invoked against them with a resounding lack of success.

The law, and the trade union which backed it, had both been openly defied in such a way that the ring-leaders went not only scot-free, but invested with a new aura in the eyes of all dissident factions.

The Order had to go, or at least to be drastically amended, and after the usual consultation between the Minister of Labour and the N.J.A.C., a new Industrial Disputes Order, 1376, was issued. The prohibition of strikes and lock-outs disappeared. There was still provision for compulsory arbitration, but obviously its appeal and usefulness would be much diminished if the arbitrament of strike or lock-out was an easy alternative. There was some acknowledgment of this anomaly in the Order; the Minister could delay reference of a dispute to the new Industrial Disputes Tribunal if he considered that either party to the dispute was resorting to coercion in some form. It was notable that the definition of a dispute in terms of the Order was now narrowed, to exclude 'a dispute as to the employment or non-employment of any person or as to whether any person should or should not be a member of any trade union'. This type of issue, which had been, and was to continue to be, frequent and troublesome, was now to be regarded as purely a domestic one, for unions and employers to deal with. Unofficial movements were not to be given cognisance; a dispute could be reported only by an employer or employers' organisation or a trade union which was party to the voluntary negotiating machinery, where such existed. The former direct obligation on employers to observe recognised terms or conditions resulting from the processes of the Order was abolished, but an 'issue' as to whether a particular employer was observing recognised terms and conditions could be reported by the appropriate organisation of employers or workers to the Minister for determination by the Tribunal. As under the previous Order, an award of the Tribunal became an implied term of the contract between the employers and workers concerned, and was legally enforceable by civil action in the courts.[11]

This Order, too, was to be regarded as 'experimental', and, since its purpose was to supplement and strengthen the voluntary machinery, it was to be subject to review at the instance of either side of industry. From the employers' point of view, it lacked even the slight appeal of the earlier Order. Strikes (like lock-outs, which, however, were rarely used nowadays by employers) were no longer forbidden, and the facility for enforcing observance of awards through the courts was clearly one of little value to employers faced with mass action. As for awards, it was not unknown for them to be rejected, not merely by dissatisfied workers, but by the union concerned, without redress for the employers. The British Employers' Confederation made no secret of its dislike, and it was no surprise when in 1958 the Conservative Minister of Labour announced that the Order was to be revoked. The T.U.C. protested, but the principle of compulsory arbitration had been gravely weakened with the watering-down of the terms of Order 1305. What was more remarkable than the decision to end its substitute was Government's apparent intention to return to its position of forty years before. It appeared that, so far as Government was concerned, neither the experience it had had thrust on it over this long and busy period of industrial relations, nor the emergence of new circumstances affecting them, had done more than to convince it that the old ideas and agencies could not be improved on, and that, above all, the maintenance of peace in industry must be left wholly to the good sense, forbearance and public spirit of the parties to industry.

After the repeal of the Order, the only survival was the provision, incorporated in the Terms and Conditions of Employment Act, 1959, to enable 'recognised terms or conditions' to be imposed on unwilling employers, through the agency of the Minister of Labour and the Industrial Court.

It was commonly argued by its critics that compulsory arbitration had had little effect on the state of industrial relations, to judge by the incidence of strikes. In the post-war years when Order 1305 was in operation, the average annual loss of time through strikes amounted to just under two million working days, which in fact had been the average ever since the depression had settled on industry in the early 'thirties; in the 'boom' years following the first War, the loss had been vastly greater. In the period immediately following the disappearance of the Order there was no significant increase in the figure, until 1955, when it went up to about 3,800,000 days, and even so it was only a little above the total for 1944, when other moral restraints were at work. In 1956 it fell again to what might be regarded as normal—around the two million mark — only to shoot up in 1957 to the highest level reached since the troubled times midway between the Wars.

The opponents of compulsory arbitration found in this record proof of its ineffectiveness. It was too facile a judgment. That the system did not appreciably diminish strikes was on the face of things true, although its deterrent effect could not be measured; but it would have been as reasonable to expect it to stop strikes as to expect the institution of a court of law to end crime. There had to be other sanctions, including discipline, through the trade unions, to habituate people to the rule of law, and above all a long process of education. The most that could be hoped for was that in time violence should cease to be regarded as an orthodox means of settling a difference of opinion, as had happened in other sectors of social relations.

It is perhaps true to say that compulsory arbitration had at least helped to foster the development of such an outlook. It was already quite pronounced in the trade union hierarchy, and owed its being to the growth, especially in the last thirty years or so, of voluntary agencies of negotiation. This was one of the main reasons for the peacefulness of the period succeeding the second War as compared with the early 'twenties. In fact, there can be no valid comparison, although it has often been attempted, since the circumstances were so vastly different. By the end of the second War, the machinery for keeping the industrial peace had improved out of all recognition, and the status of the trade unions had been enormously enhanced. Furthermore, in the second period there was infinitely less material for industrial unrest, since there was ample employment and mounting wage-rates.

The feeling, however, that it was now a 'free-for-all' certainly influenced some union leaders and their followers. There was a greater truculence, partly due to resentment at the Government's policy, which, it was argued, could contaminate the judgment of arbitrating bodies. Yet, if the major strikes of 1955 had one element in common, it was inter-union hostility. This was something which no outside authority could deal with — a stoppage due to it would not even qualify as a dispute for the purposes of Order 1376 — and it was widely held that the T.U.C. must assume authority to deal with family quarrels which upset the whole community. A move in that direction was haltingly made, and Congress authorised the General Council to use its good offices to promote a settlement in cases where negotiations seemed likely to fail and a stoppage was threatened which would involve willy-nilly members of other trade unions not concerned with the issue in dispute. It was the threat to other unions, not the menace of a strike, however unjustified, that could entitle the Council to interfere, however delicately, with the autonomy of any of its member unions.

Those who had hoped that nationalisation would usher in a new era in industrial relations were to be sadly disappointed.

The record of the coal industry under private enterprise had been notoriously bad, and both Labour politicians and trade unionists had seen in this a by-product of capitalism, and had preached for a generation at least that in state ownership lay the cure. The industry was the first to be nationalised. The relevant Act did not, however, introduce any notable innovations so far as the machinery of negotiation was concerned; this was to be worked out between the management (the Coal Board) and the Trade Union, with provision for arbitration in such cases as the parties thought proper. Roughly the same line was followed in the cases of the electricity and gas industries, and transport. There was also to be machinery for joint consultation on matters of mutual interest, including the promotion of efficiency.

In accordance with the policy previously agreed by the T.U.C. and the Labour Party, the trade unions concerned were not to be involved in management, but their special interest was acknowledged by making one of the qualifications for membership of the governing Boards 'experience of and capacity in the organisation of workers'. A trade union official was therefore always appointed, having first severed his union connections, his province being industrial relations.

This convention was no doubt designed to improve industrial relations, but in fact it was based on the assumption that they would take on a new and better character by the very act of nationalisation. Surely, it had been argued, when the profit motive ceased to be dominant — as indeed it did — the employees would expect only a reward commensurate with the productivity of their enterprise. In fact, the employees continued, logically enough, to be preoccupied with securing as great a reward as they could enforce, with if anything even less regard to the continued solvency of the enterprise than when it was under private ownership. After all, it mattered comparatively little to the worker as such whether he was working for a public Board or a private employer; his first concern was to get as good a living as possible. Furthermore, he was well aware that he was serving a statutory monopoly, which could pass on higher charges to the consumer public, even to the point of diminishing returns, since the State could and must make up losses. Nationalisation, too, meant national organisation and national responsibility; and there was a marked inclination on the part of officials, as in the Civil Service, to pass on awkward matters for decisions, which, in labour matters particularly, bred a sense of frustration on the part of those concerned.[12]

It was questionable if the fact that the former trade union officials at headquarters now had to deal with ex-colleagues served to sweeten the exchanges. The labour members of the Boards were 'poachers turned gamekeepers', and as such were bound to be somewhat suspect from the start. It was eminently sound that trade unions should make their contribution to the new administrations; but the wisdom of giving their nominees responsibility for labour matters was more doubtful. Certainly, so far as the public could judge, the course of industrial relations ran no more smoothly now than it had before. The unions were in a position of great strength. They were dealing with basic industries, so that managements and Government were more than usually anxious to avoid trouble. In the coal industry at least there was a sellers' market, with domestic consumption rationed. It was little wonder that the fact was almost lost sight of that nationalisation was intended for the benefit, not merely of the workers, but of the community. Thus, it was considered eminently reasonable that wage increases on the railways, or on London buses, should be met, in part at least, by economies in the form of curtailment of service to the public.

The coal-mining industry continued to be turbulent, a prey to 'wild-cat' strikes. In the year following nationalisation (1947), it accounted for three-fifths of all stoppages, and for two-fifths of the total time lost, nor did the record show any marked improvement in the next decade. Absenteeism, too, continued at an alarmingly high level, despite high wages, special inducements, and repeated campaigns and warnings against it.

There was one panacea for national well-being on whose
virtues trade unions, employers and Government appeared to
be in complete accord; all were agreed that greater productivity was essential to the nation's prosperity, and to an advance
in the standard of living. There might be sharp differences between workers and employers as to the respective parts to be
played by management and labour in achieving this, and as to
their respective shares of the proceeds; but these were matters
to be thrashed out in each industry, since here too there could
be no universally acceptable formula. Between the Wars the
trade union movement had laid down the policy that the unions
would work with management, and that their special knowledge should be applied to stimulate management to improve
industrial efficiency. During the War, it had become directly
associated with employers and Government in over-all planning, on bodies such as the National Production Advisory
Council and Regional Boards. It maintained this rôle in
peace-time, at the invitation of Labour and Conservative
Governments, on the Economic Planning Board, the Anglo-
American Council on Productivity, and later the British Productivity Council, and a host of other agencies.

Union leaders were convinced and, in their public utter-
ances, convincing, that both sides of industry must adapt their
old ideas to meet the challenge of the present. As in other things,
however, it was a very different matter to bring this home to the
rank-and-file, who had been nurtured in quite other doctrines.
Joint production committees had been set up at factory level
during the War, and many had survived into peace, but in most
cases they inspired little enthusiasm; they were frequently regarded by employers and union officials as at best super-
numerary to the orthodox machinery, and at worst a positive
hindrance to management.

So far the trade union side of industry was concerned, it was
essential to its conception of its place in the scheme of industry
and society that the members as a whole should appreciate the
obligation to play their full part in building up a prosperous,

dynamic economy. This would mean much more than exhortations and courses in economics for the few, although these were no doubt a useful preliminary. It would mean the strict observance of joint agreements and awards, involving an end of unofficial strikes, absenteeism and other unconstitutional behaviour; the acceptance of new machines and methods of working; the abandonment of restrictive practices; and other things entailing the renunciation of archaic attitudes deriving from other days and other ways.

The employers, too, had their responsibilities; but it was the jealously guarded prerogative of the unions to inform and lead the workers on their obligations to their own industry and to the community. By their success in performing this great task would be judged the validity of their claim to remain completely independent in pursuit of the interests of their members.

REFERENCES

1. *Trade Union Documents*, pp. 380–1.
2. B. C. ROBERTS: *National Wages Policy in War and Peace* (Allen & Unwin, 1958), pp. 36–7.
3. G. D. H. COLE: *History of the Labour Party*, pp. 438, 473;
   N. BAROU: *op. cit.*, pp. 134–5.
4. N. BAROU: p. 139 and Appendix, p. xiv;
   K. G. J. C. KNOWLES: *op. cit.*, p. 98 n;
   G. D. H. COLE: *Short History of the British Working-class Movement*, p. 484.
5. *British Trade Unionism* (P.E.P., 1955), pp. 147, 153;
   E. L. WIGHAM: *op. cit.*, pp. 183–91.
6. K. G. J. C. KNOWLES: p. 98 n.;
   Report of the Chief Registrar of Friendly Societies for 1957.
7. K. G. J. C. KNOWLES: p. 67;
   B. C. ROBERTS: *National Wages Policy in War and Peace*, p. 64.
8. B. C. ROBERTS: pp. 55–6.
9. E. L. WIGHAM: pp. 158–73;
   V. L. ALLEN: In a letter to *The Times*, 30th October, 1958.
10. *Industrial Relations Handbook* (1953), p. 134.
11. *Ibid.*, pp. 135–8.
12. R. KELF-COHEN: *op. cit.*, pp. 228–36.

CHAPTER XI

CONFLICT AND CONCILIATION

In the decade following the Second World War, the trade union movement was dominated by strong personalities, notably Arthur Deakin of the Transport and General Workers' Union, Tom Williamson of the National Union of General and Municipal Workers and Will Lawther of the National Union of Mineworkers. In 1955 these three could claim to speak on behalf of nearly two-fifths of the total union representation at the Labour Party's Annual Conference and many other unions tended to follow their lead. They worked reasonably harmoniously with the post-war Governments, not least with the Conservatives, being essentially pragmatic and moderate in their approach, both in the political and industrial spheres — thus Communists might be explicitly excluded from holding union office — and, as has been seen, as a result they had at times to demand a degree of restraint from their membership, which in some sectors was denounced as nothing short of betrayal. They were frequently assailed for their conservatism by left-wing politicians, headed by Aneurin Bevan, and constantly harassed by their own militants, who were uninhibited by considerations of national policy, and could even assert this to be a virtue by appearing, however ephemerally, as the only authentic mouthpieces of the rank and file. Whether they were condemned or ignored or condoned as manifestations of the only true industrial democracy was almost irrelevant.[1]

The late 'fifties and 'sixties saw a change in this relationship between the industrial and political organisations.[2] A degree of alienation crept in between the trade union hierarchy and the Labour Party, not primarily because of issues of doctrine, although these were to develop in the sour climate of repeated electoral failure in the three general elections of 1951, 1955 and 1959. The industrial scene on the surface seemed fairly stable; 'affluent society' came to be used as a term of reproach. A section of the Party leadership saw the ideological dedication to socialism, as embodied in Clause IV of the 1918 constitution, as an electoral liability and openly began to entertain reservations about the over-close identification of the Party with the out moded 'cloth-cap' image of the trade union movement. Hugh Gaitskell was elected Leader in 1955 and forthrightly advocated the abandonment of Clause IV, in favour of the pursuit of social policies in the context of a mixed economy. He was defeated on this issue in 1960, as well as on unilateral disarmament, by the alliance of left-wing and trade union forces, spearheaded by the new General Secretary of the Transport and General Workers', Frank Cousins. It was not surprising that the latter should have taken up a very different posture from that of his immediate predecessors. In a sense he and some of his colleagues, as in the Amalgamated Engineering Union (which, despite its craft origins, had joined the ranks of the general unions and was now next in size to the Transport and General Workers') were merely reverting to type, in that militancy, with class-war undertones, had been a feature of general unions, except for the General and Municipal Workers', since their inception, and with the return to normality it was well-nigh inevitable that there should be a recrudescence of it, even if the context had radically changed.

Gaitskell recovered from his initial defeat to win the battle for control of the Party, but was not to win the war; he died in 1963 and was succeeded by Harold Wilson, who, in the following year, led the Party back to office, albeit as a minority Government, after thirteen years in the wilderness. Although he had contested the leadership with Gaitskell, he too aimed to capture the electoral centre or 'left-of-centre', declaring emphatically that 'Government must govern' regardless of sectional interests. The emergence of a new, more ideologically

minded generation of trade union leaders also may have
stirred latent misgivings about the possible abuse of trade
union power. His Minister of Labour, Ray Gunter, a man
with an unimpeachable trade union background, addressing
a Labour Party meeting in 1951, had warned:

> ... while the unions are playing a powerful part in our
> life to-day, recognizing the astonishing restraint and state-
> manship they have shown, they are still capable of using
> power ruthlessly and denying the very essence of freedom....
> It is slily but truly said that the power of the organized
> workers is so great that they could bring down any govern-
> ment by the deliberate fostering of industrial unrest, and
> that it might well be achieved if a Conservative Government
> were elected. It is a monstrous suggestion. Political freedom
> becomes a mockery and the minority usurps power if we
> advocate the use of any means to achieve a political end.

Circumstances seemed fully to justify this challenge to trade
union political influence, at which Gaitskell had more than
hinted during his struggle with the left-wing 'bloc'. In the
late 'fifties and 'sixties the trade union movement had reached
a low point in public esteem, which is not to say that its
character had noticeably changed, rather the contrary. There
were occasional cases of flagrant trade union malpractices
which achieved notoriety. There was in particular the scandal
of the Electrical Trades Union, which became public in 1958,
and where it was ultimately proved — as in other *causes
célèbres* in trade union history, and not the last, through
individual members taking their grievances to the Courts —
that the Union's election procedures had been grossly and
fraudulently manipulated by a caucus of officials who were
associated with the Communist Party. In passing, but also
having regard to what was to transpire at a later period, it is
worth noting that no less an authority than Lord Justice
Denning declared that, even if a trade union adhered strictly
to its own rules, the judiciary 'would look upon any rule which

purported to exclude the Courts from examining and interpreting union rules as contrary to public policy and, therefore,
null and void'. There were, in short, principles of natural
justice which the Courts must uphold in defence of the individual against any form of tyranny.

An eminent academic suggested that 'one of the must
important symptoms of the year 1959 was the appearance
without raising undue commotion of two films satirising trade
union practices'; one, which was a very popular success, was
cynically entitled 'I'm All Right Jack'. In this connection it
was remarked by a political commentator that one reason
for its appeal was that the directors 'had worked within the
ethos of their time'. He wrote:

> All three parties at Westminster know the brand image of
> trade unionism has suffered ominous damage in the last
> few years. In consequence the Conservatives have at last
> lost their fear of the Unions; some Labour thinkers are
> openly rebuking them, or changing their constitutional
> entrenchments within the party; and the Liberals are
> campaigning for trade unions to be registered with the
> Registrar of Friendly Societies in such a way as to ensure
> fair elections and prevent victimisation.

He went on to quote a Socialist politician's explanation of
this poor image and the trade union movement's loss of
influence:

> 'Everyone realizes how jealously individual unions guard
> their sovereignty and how markedly this inhibits strong
> national leadership.' This, he thought, was 'certainly
> weaker than in almost any other major industrial country.
> The movement will not recover its previous high esteem
> until it can take, and substantially enforce, a clear, national
> view on such problems as the ETU, unofficial strikes,
> demarcation disputes, the rights of the individual member,
> sending to Coventry, and so on. If it fails to act, and remains

semi-ossified from however understandable a cause, one
thing is certain; a Tory Government will conveniently act
for it by setting up a Royal Commission.'³

The final conclusion was to be proved true, with, ironically
enough, one major qualification, that the Royal Commission
was to be set up by a Labour Government.

A contemporary study concluded that if Labour were in
office it would not change course any more than a Conservative
Government would if it were at odds with the demands of the
unions. The most unions could expect would be to change the
Government's methods of achieving its ends but not the
policy itself.⁴ Yet the size of the trade union movement had
increased enormously since the beginning of the century.
Then there had been 1233 trade unions with a membership
of over two million workers. The number of unions had
diminished since then, while the total membership had
increased to over ten million; by the early 'sixties there was a
formidable concentration of power, with one-half of the total
embraced by nine large unions. But too often expansion was a
matter of aggregation not rationalisation, the rule-books and
constitutions were sadly old-fashioned, methods of election
played into the hands of cliques, and policies were liable to
reflect personal ideologies more than concensus.

A popular conception of the trade union movement, as
represented by the T.U.C., was epitomised by the cartoonist
Low's delineation of it as a lumbering carthorse. It was thought
not to have kept pace with the times. Since it had been
accorded its now unique legal immunity — even the Crown
had been deprived of comparable protection by the Crown
Proceedings Act, 1947 — the milieu had been transformed.
The nature of management in private enterprise had changed
with the development of public companies, run by profes-
sionals accountable to an ever-widening circle of shareholders.
A large and vital section of industry had been vested in state-
owned corporations. This was only part of a larger and

continuing shift from the private to the public sector: by the
mid-'fifties perhaps 25 per cent of the employed population
was in the latter, which was responsible for around 50 per cent
of total investment. Employment in 'productive' industry was
contracting. The old 'boss versus worker' concept had lost
much of its validity, and the balance of power had tilted
against management. The talk now was of trade union
'bosses'.

The nature of the metamorphosis is brought out by the
Socialist politician and writer, C. A. R. (Anthony) Crosland,
in his book *The Future of Socialism*.[5] The first section, headed
'The Transformation of Capitalism', has sub-headings which
are in themselves illuminating: 'The Pre-war Power of the
Business Class', 'The Loss of Power of the Business Class to
the State', 'The Effect of Nationalisation on the Distribution
of Power', 'The Transfer of Power from Management to
Labour', etc. He effectively contrasts what he calls the pre-
1939 'subservience of the political authority . . . to the interest
of business' — with Government intervention, in so far as it
existed at all, largely directed to the support of private enterprise — with the post-war situation, when Government accepted responsibility for full employment, the rate of economic
growth, and other social and economic desiderata. Government now exerted its influence not only directly in the public
sector, but also on private enterprise through fiscal policies.
He attributes this movement mainly to the policy of full
employment and the existence of a sellers' market for labour.

There was thus a genuine dilemma confronting both governments and trade unions. The unions were faced with issues
concerning the public weal which they had not been designed
to deal with, and the solutions of which, it could be held, were
incompatible with the untrammelled exercise of their traditional rights and duties. The essential function of a union was
to fight on behalf of its own members against intransigent,
over-mighty employers, not to make common cause with other
unions, with which it might well be in rivalry, and still less

to submerge its own avowedly sectional aims in the defence of the common good or even of the 'working class' as a whole. Whatever connotation could be given the term 'working class' — and it was freely invoked in a highly emotive sense — it represented by trade union criteria a heterogeneous collection of professions, trades and occupations in which it was impossible to find a common identity, even within the one industry. Unlike its counterpart in Sweden, the movement had not developed a strong central authority, empowered to speak and act decisively on its behalf; the TUC was little more than a sounding-board for its larger members and in this respect little different from the national employers' labour organisation, the British Employers' Confederation (merged in 1965 in the Confederation of British Industry). To add to its difficulties a new phenomenon had, since the War, been insidiously but increasingly undermining the economy. This was inflation.

The phenomenon had been apparent since the War, although it had been harshly controlled in the early stages by the austere fiscal policies of Sir Stafford Cripps as Chancellor of the Exchequer. It was still relatively modest in amount, judged by later standards, and spasmodic in its progress, but it was always present. Its menace was not properly appreciated by the public, except perhaps by those sections fully exposed to it because they did not enjoy the protection of mighty trade unions, whose range now covered many 'white-collar' workers. On the whole, standards of living were improving fast: between 1951 and 1963 prices were estimated to have risen by 45 per cent, but wage-rates in the same period increased by 72 per cent. Full employment, to which all political parties subscribed, was, with some temporary setbacks, being maintained, even if an ever-increasing proportion was in local and national government. The public at this stage was more bored than frightened and there was a growing disenchantment with both the Conservatives, who had had a long spell in office (1951-64), and with Labour, who seemed hopelessly divided, as witness the famous Orpington by-election of 1962 where the Liberals won an unexpected and resounding victory.[6]

Government, too, of whatever complexion, was faced with a dilemma. Dare it interfere, against all precedent, with what was euphemistically called 'free collective bargaining'? Here it should be noted that the legal definition of a trade union, whether of employers or workers, included as one of its functions 'imposing restrictive conditions on the conduct of any trade or business'. The legal privilege thus conferred had been severely curtailed in the case of employers by the Restrictive Trade Practices Act of 1956, passed by a Conservative Government, which laid down that collusion to regulate prices or output was 'prima facie' contrary to the public interest — thus removing from employers' associations much of the immunity afforded by the Trade Disputes Act of 1906 — and appointed a Restrictive Practices Court to decide whether particular practices could, exceptionally, be tolerated. It worked very effectively, much more so than the Labour Government's Monopolies Act of 1948, which set up a Commission with powers to investigate business monopolies which appeared to threaten the public interest.

Time after time post-war administrations seeking to cure or at least alleviate the weakness of the British economy had diagnosed wage and price inflation as one of the chronic ailments. There was a growing anxiety in official quarters about the need to deal with it, as is evident from the dismal list of White Papers and legislation. Mention has been made of the Labour Government's Statement on Personal Incomes, Costs and Prices, re-issued by a Conservative Government in 1957,[7] and the establishment by the latter of the National Council on Prices, Productivity and Incomes. The Council attributed much of the blame for the unprecedented rise in the cost of living to excessive wage increases and was denounced by the Labour Opposition and the T.U.C. as politically biased. In 1961 the Government imposed a 'pay-pause' in the public sector, or at least in those parts of it directly susceptible to government control; it was held to have been breached by a settlement in the nationalised electricity supply industry — an area in which both Government and public were highly vulnerable, as had been recognised as far back as 1919. (How much more vulnerable it had become since then, with the vastly increased reliance of industry and private consumers on electricity, much of it based on coal, was yet to be demonstrated.) In 1962 the Council was abolished, but yet another White Paper appeared, 'Incomes Policy: the Next Step',[8] issued in defiance of the T.U.C., which had rejected the Government's invitation to consultations with Government, trade union representatives and employers' organisations 'to collaborate in working out suitable arrangements for maintaining a restraining influence on the levels of incomes during the next phase pending the evolution of a long-term incomes policy, with the same principles to apply to profits and dividends'. The Government went on to establish the National Incomes Commission ('Nicky'), to which particular wages issues could be referred by the contracting parties or by the Government itself.[9] Already it was being proved that this was dangerous territory; the Conservative Chancellor of the Exchequer, Selwyn Lloyd, was dismissed and *The Times* commented that he had 'more courageously than any other Conservative Chancellor . . . grasped the nettle of inflation . . . at the right place, where pressure is extorted by easy money, wage and salary rises'.[10] The T.U.C. in talks with his successor refused to have anything to do with the National Incomes Commission.

Although the new Labour Administration had a precariously narrow majority, the economic crisis demanded immediate action. The Minister for Economic Affairs, George Brown, issued a somewhat nebulous Joint Statement of Intent on Productivity, Prices and Incomes. The next year, following another White Paper, the National Incomes Commission was dissolved and replaced by the National Board for Prices and Incomes. There was to be an 'early warning system' under which proposed price and wage increases were to be referred to the Board for consideration. A National Plan was published; its central theme was the clament need to raise productivity, and it did not shrink from asserting that, while the workforce in industry as a whole must be reinforced where necessary, there also existed considerable overmanning and restrictive practices. In 1966 the Labour Party was again returned to power, this time with a comfortable margin of seats (96), and the Government passed the Prices and Incomes Act, notwithstanding the opposition of 50 Labour M.P.s and the objections of the Conservatives, who disliked the compulsory policy in principle and advocated the reform of trade union law instead. This gave the Board powers to compel wages, price and dividend increases to be submitted to it, with a right of delay of up to four months in the implementation of any particular settlement. There was a standstill on all wages, salary and dividend increases, to be followed by a further six months of 'severe restraint', and a twelve-month freeze on prices.[11]

Frank Cousins, who had been translated in 1964 from union office to a seat in the Cabinet, resigned from the Government in protest against the introduction of the measure. At the Labour Party Conference in October he predictably invoked the memory of the Tolpuddle martyrs and declared that, if the trade unions defied the Act, 'we shall be in conflict with the law. If the law is unfair, trade unionists since time immemorial have opposed the law'. It was a theme to be repeated and to be acted on under a later régime, but the Conference decided by a majority to support the Government.

Cousins returned to his Union, where he was soon to secure a redoubtable ally in Hugh Scanlon, who in 1967 became head of the Amalgamated Union of Engineering Workers. He was succeeded in office by Jack Jones, a declared adherent of the Tribune Group, in 1969, and Lawrence Daly, like Scanlon of Marxist sympathies, became Secretary of the Mineworkers' Union. The triumvirate were natural supporters of the Labour Party's Left Wing, which had already been strongly reinforced in the 1966 general election — a complete reversal of the situation in the post-war decade. In 1967 a pay and credit squeeze was imposed, accompanied by growing unemployment, but Government policy was accepted reluctantly by a conference of trade union delegates, as a temporary and unpalatable expedient. Towards the end of the year the pound was devalued and inflation was given fresh impetus. In 1968 the legislation was renewed, as part of a policy of deflation, but Labour unrest both within the House of Commons and in trade unions was mounting dangerously. At this juncture Ray Gunter resigned office as Minister of Labour, to be replaced by Mrs. Barbara Castle as Secretary of State at the newly-named Department of Employment and Productivity. There was some relaxation of the statutory code and a norm for wage and salary settlements of $2\frac{1}{2}$–$4\frac{1}{2}$ per cent was prescribed. The Government majority for the extension of the requisite legal sanctions dropped ominously to twenty-eight.

Earlier, in 1965, the Government had taken what proved to be a momentous, indeed a historic decision, since it set in motion a chain of events which was ultimately to revolutionise the relationship between the State and the unions. On his return to office as Prime Minister, Harold Wilson had declared that socialism must be modernised 'in terms of the scientific revolution . . . the Britain that is going to be re-forged in the white heat of this revolution will be no place for restrictive practices or out-dated methods on either side of industry'.[12] It was as a token of the new philosophy and especially of trade union involvement in it, that Frank Cousins had been made the first Minister of Technology. While the resort to control of incomes and prices, by consent or compulsion, might be a debatable and, at best, a transient expedient, there was no doubt that sluggish productivity was a prime factor in inflation and in Britain's uncompetitiveness. It was also plain to all that the high prices, inferior workmanship and poor delivery were in no small measure due to industrial stoppages, whoever and whatever was responsible for them.

The most disquieting features of Britain's strike record — lockouts were now almost unheard of — were not immediately apparent from the bare statistics; the annual average of lost working days between 1960 and 1965 was around three million. It had been exceeded in the past and was to be exceeded in the future. Even so, in terms of both numbers and lost output it compared poorly with that of no less than six other Western European nations; in the Netherlands, Norway, Sweden and Germany stoppages were so rare that 'no established strike pattern can be said to exist'. And the statistics did not take account of brief stoppages or the almost equally common and harmful use of overtime bans and working to rule. In one case, coal-mining, although strikes remained endemic, there was a steep decline in the number of stoppages, from 2224 in 1957 to 219 in 1968. The improvement here was partly a reflection of the fact that coal was considered to be of diminishing importance and the industry was being deliberately and progressively run down. In the same period the figure for the rest of industry rose from 635 to 2131. The real cause for alarm lay in the trends behind the statistics. Most of the stoppages were in a few key industries and were unofficial. It was not until 1960 that the Ministry of Labour began to distinguish between official and unofficial strikes, but then a rapidly deteriorating situation was revealed. In 1964–7 there were on average 82 official strikes per year, involving 84,700 workers (excluding those consequentially laid off at other establishments) and 643,000 lost working days. By contrast, the corresponding figures for unofficial stoppages were 2,125, 663,300, and 1,857,000. The figures of lost working days in relation to the total employed are usually judged to be the best measure of economic damage and here four industries had achieved a sad reputation. In the same period, the average

annual number of unofficial strikes in coal-mining was
127.7 per 100,000 with 416 lost working days per 1000 employees; shipbuilding and engineering, 45.2 and 412; motor-
vehicle manufacturing, 34.3 and 831; and the docks industry
maintained its tradition of turbulence with 65.6 stoppages and
a staggering tally of 1766 lost days. By these standards the
figures for industry as a whole, 9.2 stoppages and 84 lost days,
were modest indeed. Here it might be noted that only a
minute proportion of the disputes concerned trade union
recognition; by far the most frequent issue was wages, with
next to it 'working arrangements, rules and discipline'.[13]

This situation was bound to raise serious doubts as to the
adequacy of the industrial relations system. It meant, among
other things, that the unions in vital industries had in effect
lost control over their members. The explanations for this
phenomenon are various and inconclusive, but almost certainly one contributory factor was 'full employment', with
some industries suspected of 'hoarding' labour, and increased
social security benefits. It was no longer a problem simply
for politicians and industrial organisations; the public was
suffering as never before. A comparatively small stoppage
in one sector of the motor-manufacturing industry group
immediately had widespread repercussions on a vast area of
production, because of the inter-dependence of the various
production processes: in 1965 this group lost over 900,000
working days, not far short of one-third of the national total.
In the same way a strike in even one of the larger ports could
have quite disastrous effects on the nation's balance of payments. This key fact was well appreciated by those responsible
and it was little wonder that the Communist Party, having
consistently failed to make any impact through political
channels, should infiltrate the trade union movement as a
matter of policy. The seamen's strike of 1966 was blamed by
the Labour Prime Minister on the machinations of a 'tightly
knit group of politically motivated men ... who are now
determined to exercise back-stage pressures ... endangering

the security of the industry and the economic welfare of the nation'.[14]

It was little wonder that 'a swing in public opinion favouring greater legal intervention in industrial relations and the use of sanctions in support' was detectable. Trade union officials as a whole worked valiantly to maintain discipline within their ranks, but their position was undermined by the unceasing guerilla tactics of unofficial leaders who could start a war almost at will, knowing full well that they had no responsibility for making peace. In some unions there was a tendency on the part of officialdom to show a semblance of control by giving official cognisance to unconstitutional behaviour, to lead troops from behind, and to abdicate responsibility to shop-floor activists. The argument had a certain plausibility, since there was a valid case for giving a greater voice to workers at local, plant level. There was a genuine problem of communication, especially in the very large unions. On the other hand it could mean 'the tendency of extreme decentralisation and self-government to degenerate into indecision and anarchy'.[15] Employers were by no means guiltless, as regards both their shortcomings in management and especially their neglect of industrial relations. Too often they were willing to concede expensive settlements, since a stoppage would do grievous and possibly irretrievable damage to their operations. In a period of inflation, with a high degree of fiscal protection, many firms and industries were able to pass on increased costs, including those caused by over-manning, without undue difficulty.

It was to the credit of the Labour Government that it was the first openly to acknowledge the need for reform of industrial relations, including the law within which the system operated, and the refurbishing of philosophies and practices which had, in the main, derived from the nineteenth century. The very act of setting up a Royal Commission, in 1965, was in itself a declaration that the 'status quo' was no longer adequate to the times. The reaction of the two parties directly concerned to being put under scrutiny in this way was easily predictable in the light of past experience; any independent inquiry was in the nature of a challenge and an implied criticism and as such to be treated with hostility. This had been the traditional built-in reaction on past occasions, with rather more reason in the circumstances then prevailing, though in the event the fear of trade unions that a Royal Commission would be used as a justification for anti-union legislation had proved completely unfounded; the opposite had invariably been the case. Yet here was responsible, not a Conservative or a Liberal Government, but a Labour Government, which largely owed its existence to trade union support and in whose constitution the trade unions had a dominant place. The Government went out of its way to allay misgivings through prior consultations. The membership of the Commission, under an eminent judge, Lord Donovan, was impressive, but undoubtedly the most significant appointment was that of George Woodcock, the General Secretary of the T.U.C. He was given an almost impossible dual rôle in that, by virtue of his office, he was bound directly to represent, as no other member was, one of the two parties immediately concerned.

The terms of reference were suitably guarded to provoke the minimum of resentment, but they remained pregnant with possibilities. They were 'to consider relations between management and employees and the role of trade unions and employers' associations in promoting the interests of their members and *in accelerating the social and economic advance of the nation with particular reference to the law affecting the activities of these bodies*' (author's italics). Since the law already gave what was generally thought to be the absolute maximum of protection, and the Labour Government had in 1965, as one of its first actions, sealed the last possible loop-hole as revealed by the Rookes *v.* Barnard case (1964), any amendment of it was likely to be restrictive.

The Commission laboured mightily from 1965–8 and finally

produced a compendious and weighty report with a vast collection of useful information embodied in it, and much more attached in the very valuable research papers. For anyone who expected radical proposals, or even a systematic exposé of basic problems and remedies, it was something of a disappointment. Unlike most Royal Commissions of the kind, it referred briefly and quite inadequately to the historical background, a proper appreciation of which was an absolute precondition of any comprehension of the current problems and tasks. It did, in its Introduction, devote seven of the twenty-two paragraphs to 'Social and Economic Change since the Last Royal Commission' — an astonishingly cursory approach, since this was really its *raison d'être* and was, as it acknowledged, 'far reaching' in its implications.

The Report painstakingly highlighted the main elements of the current system of industrial relations and made useful, if somewhat cautious, observations on each of them. It did a thorough clinical examination of the anatomy, without giving much time or thought to its hereditary or genetic make-up, but was less than assured in its diagnosis of the malady, and divided on its prescriptions. Having regard to the nature of the operation and the variety of pre-conceived convictions represented on the Commission, this was to be expected. Basically it appeared to settle and concentrate on the one area of broad agreement, which was that, industrial relations having developed on a strictly voluntary basis, the right policy must be to improve this voluntary system (so far as agreement could be reached on recognition of its weaknesses) and to buttress it with the minimum of outside intervention. In this it followed the traditional attitude of its predecessors.

Perhaps, however, the most important single part of its remit, as spelt out in its terms of reference, was the question of trade union law. Not surprisingly, the Commission found 'a wide measure of agreement that the law should intervene as little as possible in what is essentially a voluntary system' and most of the members, with one outstanding dissentient (see below), endorsed this view while recognising that some amendment and, more especially, codification were essential, since the law had developed 'piece-meal' and isolated judical decisions had been followed by extemporised remedial statutes. The admirable analysis of the law governing trade unions in Chapter XIV does not explain its continuing evolutionary process, although it refers to the particular cases prompting the reforms and, curiously, does not refer to the special legislation of the two great wars, except incidentally. This is unfortunate, since the attitude of Parliament, the judiciary, and public opinion can be understood only in the light of the circumstances and motives prevailing at different times. However, the Commission seems to have assumed here, as elsewhere, that history was relatively unimportant except in so far as it entered into the actual legal judgments. The result is a lack of perspective and social context.

This major defect is severely criticised by one member, Andrew Shonfield, in his substantial Note of Reservation. No doubt having in mind the phrase in the terms of reference about the relationship between industrial relations and 'accelerating the social and economic advance of the nation', he points out that the Report 'barely concerns itself with the long-term problem of accommodating bodies with the kind of concentrated power which is possessed by trade unions to the changing future needs of an advanced industrial society.' It does not (he says) take sufficient account of the disruptive effect, in a complex economy, of the action of the few on the intricate chain of production and on the working lives of the many. He explains (as the Report does not) how the doctrine of the 'licensed conspiracy' came to be condoned by society, because of the weakness and vulnerability of the trade unions and the prejudices against them in influential quarters at critical stages of their development; during its formative period, he reminds us, trade unionism, whether among workers or employers, was regarded as a rather unpleasant but inevitable product of industrial growth, so that the law was expected to have as little to do with it as possible, lest it should appear to approve it by implication. Paragraph 5 of his Note is worth quoting in full:

It seems inconceivable in the long run that in a society which is increasingly closely-knit, where the provision of services to meet the elementary needs of a civilised daily life depends more and more on the punctual performance of interrelated work tasks of a collective character, trade unions will be treated as if they had the right to be exempt from all but the most rudimentary legal obligations. This is the traditional view, which has bitten deep into the British system of industrial relations. It is what the T.U.C. in their evidence to the Royal Commission referred to as the principle of 'abstention, of formal indifference' on the part of the State.

Accordingly, he is led to condemn the principle, which the Commission as a whole accepts as characteristic of the British system, that collective bargaining should remain outside the law, starting off with the proposition that such 'abstention' on the part of the law 'from the activities of mighty subjects tends to diminish the liberty of the ordinary citizen and to place his welfare at risk'.

Divergences on this crucial issue of principle, expressed in isolation by Andrew Shonfield, manifest themselves in various places in the Report, and the attempt to reconcile divergent views on it explain what may be seen as a lack of coherence in its conclusions. The protective legislation enacted between 1871 and 1965 was to be maintained, with certain modifications. The blanket immunity from civil action given in Section 4 of the 1906 Act should, as was certainly the original intention, be confined to trade disputes. Since 351 trade unions, representing 85 per cent of trade union membership, were already voluntarily registered by the Registrar of Friendly Societies, incurring certain obligations and enjoying certain advantages as a result, it was eminently reasonable that trade unions and employers' associations should be given corporate personality with 'concomitant liability to register in a new Register of Trade Unions and Employers' Associations'. Registration would not be compulsory, since non-recognition as a trade union would be sufficient inducement, and most unions already registered, not only as an administrative and legal convenience but as 'evidence to the public that the trade union is a stable organisation desirous of conforming to good standards of administration'. Nevertheless, persistent and wilful breach of collective agreements was not to lead automatically to deregistration, an awkward posture from which a substantial minority of the Commission dissociated themselves. This posture Lord Donovan attempts not very convincingly to explain in his somewhat apologetic Addendum: deregistration might mean deprivation of the immunity from civil action conferred by Section 4 of the 1906 Act (which some might regard as logical) but also it 'would seem less than just until the system of industrial relations is reformed so as to give unions the requisite degree of control of the situation' — whatever this meant.

By a majority the Commission found that only bodies so registered should be entitled to the protection of the first limb of Section 3 of the 1906 Act, which provided that no action could be brought against any person inducing another to break his contract in contemplation or furtherance of a trade dispute. The effect, it was thought by its supporters, would be to deter unofficial strikes. The minority, including George Woodcock, resisted it on the same grounds, arguing that it would leave unofficial strikers 'exposed' and that the removal of their immunity was unjustifiable and incompatible with the (extensive) proposals for reform of the voluntary system.

There was to be a single comprehensive Act of Parliament, under which a Commission on Industrial Relations was to be established. It should have attached to it an Industrial Law Committee to keep the new legislation under review. The

Commission, a full-time body, was to investigate issues referred to it by the Department, including cases arising out of collective agreements registered with it, and such registration was to be immediately obligatory for companies over a certain size. Its decisions in such cases were not, however, to be mandatory and there were to be no penalties for non-compliance with its recommendations. It was not to concern itself with an incomes policy, which, if it existed, was a Government responsibility. The jurisdiction of the Industrial Court would be extended and strengthened and industrial tribunals would become labour tribunals with enlarged scope.

To judge by the outcome, it would seem that the Report had not provided the clear-cut answers which had been hoped for, by some at least of the most influential members of the Cabinet. This, of course, was not an unusual experience so far as Royal Commissions dealing with trade unions (or other matters) were concerned. The Government did not take refuge in the recesses of the Report. On the contrary, it appeared to reject its central thesis that Government should maintain its traditional rôle of non-intervention and that industrial relations should remain, as far as possible, outside the scope of the law.

In 1969 a White Paper was issued, 'In Place of Strife'.[16] The promise of this title was more than fulfilled in what must surely rank as one of the most lucid and incisive exposés of an extremely complex problem. It was, of course, of necessity very brief but, within its limited compass, it achieved a remarkable feat of compression allied with intelligent selectivity. It succeeded, where the Commission had signally failed, in showing the wood instead of the trees and, what was equally important, in showing the landscape in which the wood had grown. There was none of the repeated equivocation and qualification which had marked the Royal Commission's Report: this was a brisk, uncompromising presentation of weaknesses and remedies. The White Paper, too, did what the

Government had asked the Royal Commission to do: it put the emphasis squarely on the public interest and not on the sanctity of bipartite voluntary collective bargaining. And in its conclusions, while making courteous acknowledgement from time to time of the Commission's labours, it was manifest that the Government was prepared to go much further than the Report in regard to policy.

The White Paper opened with a surprisingly severe condemnation of important elements in the existing system of industrial relations, which, it said, quite failed to prevent injustice, disruption of working and inefficient use of manpower. Management was harshly — and justly — criticised on the grounds, among others, that at times employers were 'able unfairly to exploit the consumer and endanger economic prosperity'. There was (it stated) need for new and radical legislation, and proposals were based on two main grounds:

(1)   'to help contain the disruptive expression of industrial conflict' and to safeguard not only those directly involved but the community at large, and

(2)   to ensure acceptance without reservation of the principle that the necessary reforms could not be achieved without 'the active support and intervention of Government'.

Nobody with a sense of responsibility had denied that there were things wrong with industrial relations: the big issue before the Commission had been and remained to what extent, if at all, these things could be corrected or improved by Governmental interference. This issue is dealt with at some length in paragraph 5 and puts the situation into historical perspective. First it exposed the scarecrow, which had so often been used to frighten off intruders, that voluntaryism was the essence of industrial relations and that this was a field to be preserved for employers and trade unions. It reminded that 'the State has always been involved in the process of industrial relations. It has always had to provide a framework of law'. So much for the legend that industrial relations had been entirely self-generating and had had continually to fight outside forces, including government. The State's responsibility having been categorically affirmed, the only question then was how best this responsibility was to be discharged. The White Paper freely admitted that there were in this matter, as evidenced in the proceedings of the Royal Commission and in Parliament, 'two conflicting philosophies'. The first was the doctrine of 'collective laissez-faire', that is, the freedom of the two parties (workers and employers) to settle their mutual affairs with a minimum of Governmental and legal restraint. The second was the view that the State must act where necessary 'to contain disruptive consequences of the struggle for those not immediately affected', especially where there was a threat to the interests of the community, or where social and economic objectives were being frustrated by collective bargaining. The White Paper referred to some of the ways in which the State had intervened for close on a century, from the restrictions in the 1875 Act on strike action in certain circumstances, to the benefits to employees of the (Conservative) Contracts of Employment Act and the (Labour) Redundancy Payments Scheme. It pushed home this point with a reference to the demand both from employers, as for instance for anti-strike legislation, and from trade unions, for minimum wages and the statutory enforcement of trade union recognition, for State regulation — 'at least', it added dryly, 'where they see it as advantageous to them'.

The document proceeded to summarise the existing situation as the Government saw it, and again it pulled no punches. It drew attention to the displacement of labour by business mergers and to the fact, contributed to by amalgamations and by fiscal protection, that 'imperfect competition in many industries may enable unions and employers to combine to exploit their market power at the expense of the community'. Here was a complaint against monopolistic organisations which had been voiced for centuries, and, significantly enough, most bitterly when combinations of workers and employers first began to emerge in a recognisable form as far back as the sixteenth century. Like Andrew Shonfield, in his Note of Reservation to the Report of the Royal Commission, it emphasised that 'the growing interdependency of modern industry means that the use of the strike weapon in certain circumstances can inflict disproportionate harm on the rest of society . . . strikes by groups in key positions can damage the interests of other people so seriously that they should only be resorted to when all other alternatives have failed'. Here again was a stricture on so-called militancy — i.e. the precipitate resort to industrial action whether official or unofficial. It both identified and condemned the acknowledged malaise in industrial society, which had inspired the Government's enquiry in the first place. The weakness of the statistics so often produced by those who condoned this malaise was also underlined; they were 'a very imperfect measure' of the economic consequences. The number of strikes had been increasing of recent years, and, what was more, the 'typical British strike' was unofficial and might be held, not only in defiance of the responsible trade union or unions, but in complete disregard of its consequences for the community. It is interesting to observe how the White Paper returns time and again to this theme of the good of society and the fact that it might be imperilled by the concerted actions of employers or workers.

Employers were given their full share of blame, especially for their arbitrary behaviour, and indeed were told, as they had been told by the Royal Commission, that they must accept major responsibility for reform of the system. The fault, however, must be shared with labour. There were, for instance, the 'chaotic and inflationary shopfloor pressures'. This was a side-swipe at the shop steward movement in so far as it was not controlled by the trade unions. Finally, the White Paper made the very important point that the troubles had been exacerbated by the fact that Britain was passing through a phase of exceptionally rapid technological change, which required the constant adaptation of techniques, in industrial relations as in other departments of production.

The policy set out in the White Paper, in the light of this penetrating analysis, was therefore to be four-pronged. There was to be reform of the system of collective bargaining from within; there were to be new extraneous aids to supplement self-help; there was to be an extension of the rôle and rights of trade unions, which in the new definition proposed, as in the Report, was to mean only organisations of workers; and there were to be 'new safeguards for the community and individuals'. To fill 'a major gap in the public apparatus for change', a Commission on Industrial Relations was to be established, without judicial authority or legal sanctions to back up its decisions. However — and this was not the only instance of *reculer pour mieux sauter* — there was a quite dramatic departure from the Commission's recommendations in this area by the proposed establishment of a new Industrial Board. This would deal with disputes and would be endowed with powers, through what came to be called pejoratively 'the penal clauses', to impose financial penalties for disobedience of its decisions on an employer, a trade union or individual offenders. The fines would be recoverable through civil remedies. The Government was obviously not greatly impressed by the Commission's conclusions, or those of its Chairman, on the difficulty of applying such legal sanctions, and indeed the Commission had based its case almost wholly on the notorious Betteshanger Colliery case during the Second War, where the imposition of mass fines for breach of the law on strike action had degenerated into a fiasco.

The majority recommendation of the Royal Commission that Section 4 of the 1871 Act, which precluded the legal enforcement of agreements, should be repealed, was accepted, although the Government declared itself against making collective agreements legally binding as a principle; the parties could, however, if willing, give legal force to an agreement by saying so in writing.

The Government flatly rejected, on the other hand, the much more important majority recommendation that the protection of Section 3 of the 1906 Act be restricted to registered trade unions; but at the same time trade unions would be required to register with a new Registrar of Trade Unions and Employers' Associations under pain of financial penalty, so it would appear that very much the same end would be attained and by a better method. The White Paper insisted that the trade union movement needed to be modernised in various ways, including by amalgamation, and it went further than the Royal Commission in promising grants and loans for this purpose, even to the T.U.C. There was another major departure from the Commission's recommendations in that the Minister was to be empowered to impose by Order a 'conciliation pause' of twenty-eight days' duration where joint procedures had not been exhausted, if the threatened stoppages were likely to have serious repercussions; again there would be financial penalties for breach of such an Order. It was agreed that Section 4 of the 1906 Act gave an unrealistic spread of immunity to trade unions and that this immunity should be confined to the circumstances of a trade dispute.

There was much more that was noteworthy in the White Paper, in the way of proposals as well as observations. In the latter category one might be singled out: that traditional areas of trade unionism — notably mines, railways and docks, which, of course, at one time were the key sectors of the economy — had declined in size, while other areas, especially in white-collar employment, had been steadily increasing; one result had been that the proportion of the total labour force belonging to trade unions had actually contracted in the last few years and this would presumably be a continuing development. The implications of this for the trade union movement were not referred to, but in fact they could hardly be over-stated.

'In Place of Strife' was a towering land-mark. It officially declared an end to the State policy, as it had evolved over a century at least, of dissociating itself from industrial relations except in so far as it was required to do so at the instance of the parties themselves, or because employers and workers had not sufficiently organised themselves for purposes of collective bargaining. It needed courage of a high order to breach the conventions which had become entrenched over this long period and, in particular, the central assumption that industrial relations were the private concern of industry. It was thus bound to evoke furious reactions, especially from the trade unions, and not least because it came from a Labour Government. Even so, the organised uproar which ensued exceeded all reasonable anticipations, as did the political repercussions.

The T.U.C., already smarting under the incomes policy, was bitterly and openly resentful of the strictures and implications of the White Paper (the C.B.I. hardly less so), describing the proposals as 'misguided, unacceptable and unworkable', while Jack Jones, General Secretary-elect of the Transport Workers', denounced the idea of 'bureaucratic state intervention'. Many Labour M.P.s were equally hostile. There was little objection to a Commission on Industrial Relations, which was duly established in January, 1969, any trade union misgivings being further allayed by the appointment as its chairman of George Woodcock and by its innocuous, but potentially constructive, remit: 'to examine matters referred to it by the Secretary of State for Employment and Productivity on issues of industrial relations, to promote improvements and to report'. In March the White Paper was submitted to the Commons as a basis for legislation, and no fewer than 55 Labour M.P.s opposed the motion, while another 40 aligned themselves with the Conservatives in abstaining. The National Executive Committee of the Labour Party rejected the policy by a majority of over three to one and was not assuaged by Mrs. Castle's reassurances. Nevertheless the Government

announced its intention of introducing the necessary legislation, the main features of which were to be the right to
impose a 28-day 'conciliation pause' in important unconstitutional strikes, and the creation of an Industrial Board,
presided over by an independent legal chairman, to administer
the law, with power to levy financial penalties for breach of
its provisions; the penalties would be enforceable in the civil
courts through attachment of earnings. The Prime Minister
declared that the message of the Bill was 'essential to the
Government's continuing in office'.[17] The clamour rose to a
crescendo and a nation-wide labour campaign, official and
unofficial, was mounted. Over 100,000 took part in a May
Day strike, which shut down the newspapers. The total of
working days lost during 1969 rose by nearly 50 per cent.
The T.U.C. made little effort to restrain the unrest although
its own outrage was ventilated by constitutional means. It
convened a special Congress, the first since 1920, and in May
published its own 'Programme for Action', which pledged
it to discourage by persuasion unofficial and inter-union
disputes, in return for the abandonment of legal sanctions.
Faced with such unyielding resistance and with a revolt in its
Parliamentary rank and file, not to mention well-leaked divi-
sions within the Cabinet and the imminent prospect of a
general election, a hasty series of meetings between the
Prime Minister and Mrs. Castle and T.U.C. representatives,
including Jack Jones and Hugh Scanlon, took place in May.
They were resumed following the special Congress on 5th
June, which overwhelmingly endorsed the 'Programme'. A
settlement was reached on 18th June and announced by the
Prime Minister to the Commons next day. In return for the
T.U.C.'s 'solemn and binding undertaking' to intervene as
necessary to put such pressure as it could on its members to
avoid unofficial action, the Government had decided to
renounce its proposals to introduce legal sanctions. The
incomes policy was also in ruins as a result of industrial
militancy, especially in the public sector.

The Conservative Party had quite unequivocally committed itself to a thorough-going reform of industrial relations while in opposition and in the closing stages of the Parliamentary debate had undertaken to create a 'fresh, clear, comprehensive framework of civil law to make a more favourable environment for change, to buttress responsible action and to provide some deterrent to the small irresponsible minority'.[18] Withdrawal by the Labour Government of its policy could be denounced politically both on the grounds that it meant the abandonment of its commitment to radical change, and that this withdrawal represented a defeat of Government by the vested interests of trade unionism. It could be construed as an abdication by the State of its responsibilities, categorically acknowledged in the Government's own White Paper, for effective participation in and regulation and regularisation of the industrial relations system, for the good of society as a whole. There was therefore, an easy electoral advantage gained; but the Conservative Party also reckoned that public opinion had welcomed the Labour Government's initial resoluteness in this matter and was disappointed and disillusioned by its surrender (as it might appear) to the T.U.C. The public, too was shocked by the display of extra-Parliamentary force in opposition to Government, much of it at the behest of the more militant trade union leaders and much of it clearly used as a medium by elements which had little or nothing in common with the trade union movement. The unions' lack of co-operation with the Labour Government's anti-inflation policy, of which the White Paper could be seen as a part, was assailed, sometimes with too little perception, by many socialists. After the general election, Lord Balogh, who had been Economic Adviser to the Government and Consultant to the Prime Minister, passed the severest strictures on the whole ethos of the trade union movement as at present constituted. He attributed a large share of responsibility for the failure to reconcile full employment with expansion and stability to its 'incomprehension and resistance', charged its organisation with being 'monopolistic and bureaucratic', thought 'free' collective bargaining encouraged social inequality (echoing Sidney Webb's verdict that sections gained for themselves advantages 'over the less fortunate of their comrades') and warned that 'when trade union leaders threatened to thwart the Chancellor's policy by further wage demands, they challenged a fundamental constitutional principle, the principle that parliament only can decide through the government which it supports . . . it is based on a complete misunderstanding of the relative power of unions and the government'. He concluded that the T.U.C. and the unions were risking retaliatory Government measures, 'not without the approval of a considerable portion of the voters', or, 'more honourably, there might be a fierce clash of will in which the unions might (as in France) not come out victorious'.[19]

Had the T.U.C. been given statutory authority to impose reform on the trade unions, the reaction might have been less strong, but there was no such suggestion, for the very good reason that the trade unions would have none of it. That there were those in the T.U.C. who genuinely wanted reform from within could not be in any doubt — the executive had been seeking off and on to strengthen its own powers *vis-à-vis* its constituents over many years — but the Labour Government's final stand was that the T.U.C. had declared its acceptance of a moral responsibility for the better conduct of industrial relations and that this declaration must be taken as fulfilling the intentions of the proposed legislation so far as enforcement of a code of constitutional behaviour was concerned. This was patently an absurd assumption, since experience had demonstrated that individual unions, especially the most powerful, would not tolerate interference from a central body. The 'solemn and binding' undertaking proved to be no more than a pious repetition of the abortive 'Declaration of Intent' of 1964.

It was not surprising, then, that reform of the industrial

relations system was one of the principal planks in the Conservative Party's election programme. It was the first time in history this had happened, unless one includes the still-born 'Industrial Charter' of 1947.[20] The policy had not figured in the Labour manifestos in 1964 and 1966, so this was something of a challenge to the electorate. How far it improved the Conservatives' electoral prospects must remain a matter of debate, but quite evidently it did them no harm, and its appeal was enhanced by the worsening strike situation. Whatever the reasons, the Conservative Party was returned to power in 1970, in a dramatic shift of public opinion which confounded the psephological pundits, and with an unmistakable mandate to deal with the problems of labour unrest on definite lines. There was no hesitancy to do so; indeed, action was initiated with such immediacy and in such a form as to give fresh ammunition to the massed battalions which had fought and defeated the Labour Government, and which now re-formed, only to find themselves confronted with an administration much less amenable to labour pressures. The new cry was that the Government was out to 'bash the trade unions', but it was no easy thing to mount a fresh attack over much the same ground and with similar tactics, against an opponent prepared for it.

The Government's plan had already been formulated and was made public on 5th October, 1970, when the Secretary for the Department of Employment published a document headed 'The Industrial Relations Bill: A Consultative Document'. In spite of its title there was no attempt as in 'In Place of Strife' at persuasion. This would perhaps have been a work of supererogation, since after 'In Place of Strife' and the debates which had already taken place in and out of Parliament, the discussion was almost bound to be sterile. The main issues had been identified and the protagonists had taken up positions. Not the least significant feature of the Document was that, although purporting to serve as a basis in consultations with the T.U.C. and the C.B.I., it gave notice that views from these or other interests must be submitted not later than 13th November, and it was made clear that the Government would in any case adhere to its chief formulae. The T.U.C. refused to be drawn into talks, and it and other opponents of the measures girded themselves for battle, in Parliament, in the workplace and in the streets. Yet the outcome was almost certain from the start. Demonstrations and industrial action to 'kill the Bill' were on a massive scale and caused much disruption. There were even demands in some quarters for a general strike, but the idea seems never to have been seriously entertained by the T.U.C.; it did sponsor a national one-day stoppage in protest, only to reject the suggestion of further action of the sort at a special conference. Some of its members were less inhibited; the Engineering Union organised a one-day strike which involved about $1\frac{1}{4}$ million workers and stopped the national press. It is doubtful if these stoppages, official and unofficial, generated any public sympathy. The real battle was fought in Parliament, where the Government was able to exploit not only a secure majority, and the device of the guillotine to curtail what could have been an interminable debate, but also the record in this field of the Opposition when in office. The Opposition's leading speaker was Mrs. Castle, who had been responsible for 'In Place of Strife' and had argued so eloquently and forcefully for far-reaching reform, and whose denunciations of the new Bill were therefore bound to be received with considerable scepticism even by her own back-benchers, as well as by trade unionists. In their essentials the Consultative Document and the Industrial Relations Bill which quickly followed it had much in common with the Labour Government's original approach, but were a good deal more uncompromising and exhaustive, although in some respects less authoritarian. The Bill became law in August, 1971.

A legal distinction was drawn between trade unions and employers' associations, but, to qualify for these titles and for the benefits of the Act, organisations of employers and workers had to be registered, and their special character was recognised in the creation of the new post of Registrar of Trade Unions and Employers' Associations. Applicants for registration must satisfy the Registrar that their constitution and rules conformed with a fairly rigorous set of criteria, whereas previously the requirements had been in very general terms. Registration would confer corporate status, a provision recommended by the Royal Commission but rejected in the Labour Government's White Paper. In the light of the statutory obligations imposed, however, this was of much less significance than under the 'status quo'. Even an unregistered organisation could be sued in its own name under the Act. There were substantial compensations for registration, in the way of ability to demand union recognition and bargaining rights of various sorts, the continued exemption from tax of funds devoted to provident benefits, as well as safeguards for individuals from arbitrary treatment by employers or unions, and so on; but perhaps the outstanding feature from the point of view of this narrative was that the immunity from civil liability conferred by the new legislation was confined to registered organisations, taking industrial action in pursuance of trade disputes, which themselves were subject to restrictive definitions. This removed at a stroke the blanket immunity given under the 1875 and, more particularly, the 1906 Acts and so went much further than the recommendations of the Royal Commission and the late Government's proposals, although both had agreed that some limitation was desirable and that unions should be required to register and submit their rules for approval. What was novel and more galling to the unions was the enumeration of 'unfair practices', applying to both employers and workers, an area which was highly sensitive and which did not lend itself to simple prescription; these would be illegal whether or not the organisations concerned were registered. The right to withdraw labour, with due notice, remained untouched so long as it was not in support of an 'unfair industrial practice'; but inducement to

breach of contract was allowed only to a registered organisation. This would hit, and was intended to do so, at unofficial
'lightning' strikes. Industrial action against 'an extraneous
party' not directly involved in the dispute, i.e. 'blacking',
would rank as an 'unfair practice'; this ruled out certain
forms of sympathetic action. Inter-union disputes and political
strikes were also put outside the law. There must be no
compulsion to join a union and the 'closed shop' was outlawed
(save in very exceptional cases) and jointly agreed 'agency
shops' substituted.

There were provisions where the difference between the
Labour Government's treatment and that of the Conservative Government was in emphasis rather than in substance.
Thus the former had declared its objection in principle to
making collective agreements legally binding but had conceded that the 1871 Act, in so far as it presented an impediment
to such agreements, should be modified to allow the parties to
enter into legally enforceable contracts if they both wished;
under the Act a collective agreement would be a legal contract
unless it contained provision to the contrary. The Labour
Government, going against the Commission's conclusion, had
wanted a 'conciliation pause' in cases where the Secretary of
State decided that the conventional procedures had not been
exhausted or where a strike was likely to have serious effects,
the maximum duration of the truce to be 28 days, with financial
penalties for breach of the order; the Conservative Government followed the same lines, except that the maximum
period was to be 60 days. On the question of ballots before
strike action, the Labour Government, while agreeing in
principle with the Commission's dismissal of the requirement,
had proposed that the Secretary of State should have authority
to require a ballot of trade union members where a strike, in
his opinion, presented a threat to the economy or the public
interest; the Conservative Government authorised the Secretary of State in such circumstances to apply to the Industrial
Court for an order requiring a ballot.

Taking the legislation as a whole, its importance lay in its dual approach to the whole problem of industrial relations. In the first place, there was to be a tightening and codification of the law, with weighty sanctions; for example, swingeing fines could be levied, related to the size and presumable wealth of the trade union or association concerned, or without limit where unregistered organisations were involved, and damages could be awarded. Secondly, there was the policy that, so far as this could be done without prejudice to normal access to the established courts of law, industrial relations should be regarded as a special area with its own corpus of legislation and with new machinery for its operation, which would have an exclusive jurisdiction over civil cases arising from industrial disputes. So 'Enactments Repealed' listed the whole of the 1871 Act, substantial parts of the 1875 Act, the whole of the Trade Union Amendment Act 1876, the whole of the 1906 Act, and the whole of the Trade Disputes Act, 1965.

The enforcement of the code of law and the associated code of good practice which was to go with it, was to be secured through special bodies newly established for the purpose, or existing agencies suitably reinforced. Here again the Conservative Government was broadly in agreement with its predecessor, but the apparatus was more formidable. There was to be a National Industrial Relations Court, to be called the Industrial Court, with the status of a High Court. Since it was to discharge a judicial function and other courts were debarred from dealing with legal issues arising from the Act, the President was to be a judge, while the other judicial and lay members were to be appointed by the Crown on the joint recommendation of the Lord Chancellor and Secretary of State. The tribunals already established under the Industrial Training Act, 1964, were to have additional duties. The existing Commission on Industrial Relations was to be reconstituted as a statutory body, to deal with issues, general or particular, referred to it by the Secretary or the Court.

Finally, there was to be an Industrial Arbitration Board, to take the place of the Industrial Court established by the Act of 1919, with powers of compulsory arbitration more extensive than hitherto.

The special T.U.C. conference held in March, 1971, had pledged its membership to a policy of non-cooperation in the implementation of the Act when passed, by refusing to register or remain registered, or to serve on the N.I.R.C. or C.I.R., and this policy was more than endorsed by the annual Congress, with the adoption of a motion by Hugh Scanlon to make it mandatory. The majorities on each occasion were much narrower than might have been expected, reflecting the reluctance of many to put themselves outside the law and thereby forfeit valuable benefits. The T.U.C. instruction which followed was rejected by some important unions, including the National Union of Seamen, the first to be disciplined as a result. A year hence, in March, 1972, 146 unions had formally asked for their registration to be cancelled; although this was under 30 per cent of the total, it represented over 60 per cent of the membership.[21] In September of that year the Congress suspended 32, later reduced to 20, as penalty for their obduracy.

The first real challenge, however, was unofficial and, not surprisingly, came from within the docks industry, largely the province of the Transport and General Workers' Union. The spread of 'containerisation' methods of packing goods had expedited traffic through the docks and the resultant contraction of dock work, as defined in the statutory Dock Labour Scheme, was resented by dock workers. They resorted to 'blacking' employers, now an 'unfair industrial practice', and several of the companies affected sought the protection of the Industrial Court. The Transport and General Workers' Union, in accordance with the views of its leadership and the dictates of the T.U.C., was not represented in Court, at the first hearing in March, 1972, and, as the 'blacking' continued, was fined £5000 with a warning that, if it persisted in its 'contempt', it was liable to sequestration of its assets, without limit. A further fine of £50,000 followed. Both fines were paid and the T.U.C. relaxed its previous ruling, to allow its members to appear before the judicial authorities under the Act. On appeal, the House of Lords sustained the Industrial Court's decision, against a ruling by the Court of Appeal, and confirmed that the Union must be held responsible for the actions of its shop stewards. Another case, emanating from Hull, also went to the House of Lords, with the same outcome. Officially the Union was now trying, belatedly and with little success, to impose order on its unruly element; the unofficial action developed into a campaign, and a climax was reached when seven men were arraigned before the Court, at the instance of a cold storage company outside the ambit of the Dock Labour Scheme, which was being picketed, and five were ordered to desist. They defied the order and were committed to prison for 'contempt'. It was blatantly evident that this was their aim, and it was condemned as self-sought 'martyrdom' by no less a person than the Shadow Secretary for Employment. But it served its purpose; there was uproar in the docks and other industries, and the T.U.C. General Council called a one-day national strike for 26th July. On that day, however, the five were released, against their will, on the application to the Industrial Court of the Official Solicitor, acting as a providential *deus ex machina*, on the grounds that, as the House of Lords had that day established, the Act should be enforced against organisations rather than individuals.[22]

Frontal assaults of this nature were hailed by militants, including politicians, as triumphs against an unjust law; they also demonstrated union lack of control over their members. More effective and less offensive means were to hand. Early in 1971 the Government had abolished the Prices and Incomes Board as token of its abandonment of statutory constraint, but was faced with mounting inflation, fuelled partly by its own economic policies and partly by excessive wage demands, backed with industrial action. In the two years up to April, 1972, average earnings rose by 25 per cent, as against a prices increase of 16 per cent. The first official national coal strike since 1926, in January/February, over a wages dispute, hit industry and the public with paralysing force, because it was accompanied by ferocious picketing of coal-fired power stations, and a state of emergency was declared. It ended in wholesale concessions to the miners by a court of inquiry. In March the Government initiated a series of discussions with the T.U.C. and the C.B.I. on the problem of inflation. Neither of these bodies favoured statutory controls, and the T.U.C. insisted on a package deal, including the repeal, or at least the suspension, of the Industrial Relations Act. The Prime Minister was equally adamant that this, in common with certain other issues raised by the T.U.C. such as entry to the European Economic Community (a subject over which the T.U.C. remained stubbornly insular at all times), was the prerogative of Parliament. He offered an undertaking that the Act would be reviewed 'after a proper period of operation'. An official national dock strike started towards the end of July, also over wages, and again a state of emergency was proclaimed. The tripartite discussions finally broke down in November, after ten meetings, and the Government introduced a statutory programme, starting off with a 90-day freeze on pay, prices, dividends and rents.[23] It was opposed by the Labour Opposition, which accused the Government of 'deliberate alienation of the trade unions'. The T.U.C., for its part, in effect broke off diplomatic relations with the Government by a declaration of its General Council in January, 1973; refused to co-operate with the Pay Board and Prices Commission, established under the second stage of the policy introduced in April; and sponsored a national day of protest on May Day. It had also entered, a year earlier, into a close communion with the Labour Opposition, through a liaison committee: this produced a joint statement which laid down the framework of policy for a future Labour Government. Not only did it utterly repudiate the concept of compulsion in relation to trade union activities; it guaranteed them a much larger rôle in social and economic affairs than they could have achieved by 'free' collective bargaining, through 'industrial democracy' enforced by legislation. The T.U.C. and the Labour Party, the latter chastened by bitter experience of confrontation with its old ally, had entered into a binding and public concordat, whose terms had patently been dictated by the T.U.C.[24]

In the event, the reaction of most unions, always excepting the Engineering Union, proved less implacable than that of the T.U.C. There was, of course, industrial action on the wages front, in support of the inevitable 'special cases', but there was also a wide recognition that the formula for the second stage — a flat award along with a percentage increase and a modest maximum total — gave the greater benefits to the lower paid. The mood of the rank and file seemed receptive to the call for restraint. Even the miners rejected by ballot their executive's invitation to call a national stoppage in support of their claim, and the pay code was well observed. A much more sophisticated formula was prescribed for Stage 3 to follow in November, 1973, with a choice between a more generous scale of flat award and percentage increases, and it introduced the principle of a cost of living 'threshold' (7 per cent), beyond which further increments were permissible, as well as compensation for 'anti-social' hours. This was a much more flexible arrangement, giving a good deal of scope for domestic negotiation.

For the first time a national prices and incomes policy was being systematically evolved, as a long-term measure and not as a panic reaction. Both sides of industry chafed at its restrictions and in-built anomalies, but its prospects of commanding a reluctant acquiescence looked fairly promising. By the end of 1973, there had been 550 settlements under Stage 3, covering 4 million workers.[25] There were squalls, but they did not seem to presage a hurricane. Despite the dispensation accorded by the T.U.C., the Amalgamated Union of Engineering Workers refused even to appear before the Industrial Court, in 1972, to answer a complaint of unreasonably refusing re-admission to an ex-member, disregarded the Court's order, and was fined £5000 for 'contempt', with, on its refusal to pay, the issue of writs of sequestration and the award against it of costs. Continued defiance led to a fine of £50,000, with up to £5000 costs, and this was duly levied on its assets. In another case, started in September, 1973, the Union proved equally contumacious, was even more heavily fined, ordered to pay substantial compensation to the company concerned, and, on its refusal to pay or even to appear before the Court, had the bulk of its assets sequestrated. A Labour motion in Parliament called for the dismissal of the President of the Court and the Union called a national strike, but this was abandoned after the mysterious payment by an anonymous donor of £65,000 to discharge the Union's debt.

There were more ugly manifestations of militancy. The example of brute violence set in the miners' strike in 1972 had not been lost on the agitators. In the course of a building workers' strike, a number of men were convicted and imprisoned at Shrewsbury on charges of gross intimidation, and the discreditable myth of the 'Shrewsbury martyrs' was conceived. Then, towards the end of 1973, a combination of events transformed the whole industrial and political scene.

The 1972 court of inquiry into the miners' claim had found that their wages had lost ground relatively to those of other industries and that this anomaly should be rectified by 'wholly exceptional' treatment; this was duly accorded. Towards the end of 1973 the National Union of Mineworkers imposed an overtime ban to enforce a claim far in excess of the most generous interpretation of the 'pay code', although it was widely believed that Stage 3 had been expressly framed to accommodate the miners' case. This alone might have been tolerable — in fact it endured for some three months — but a completely unforeseen and unforeseeable factor suddenly appeared. The Arab–Israeli war in October, 1973, led to a drastic cutback by the Middle East oil producers, and savage and repeated price rises rocked the economies of the West, not least that of Britain. The curtailment of both coal and oil supplies to the power-stations necessitated the declaration of a state of emergency in November, and, to make matters even worse, the rail drivers' union, ASLEF, and the Electrical Power Engineers' Association resorted to industrial action in support of wage claims. To conserve electricity supplies the Government, in December, 1973, decreed a three-day week for industry. (It was a sad comment on normal standards of productivity that in many instances output fell by far less than the reduction in working-hours, thanks to the response of both managements and workers). The Government still rejected the view that the miners' case should again constitute an 'exception', and were not impressed by the bland assurance of the T.U.C. that a settlement in breach of the official limits would not be used as an argument by other unions. In February, 1974, the N.U.M., after a ballot (required by its rules) which gave it authority to step up industrial action, called an all-out national strike.

Some of its spokesmen left no doubt that the strike was, to say the least, quasi-political. The Vice-President, a Communist, made a public speech, in which he was reported as seeking 'a recall of the T.U.C. to mobilise the unions to burst Phase 3, to defeat the Tory Government, and to elect a Labour Government committed to left progressive policies'.[26] And even this, it was suggested in some trade union quarters, would be only an interim political move towards the 'socialist' state. While the official Labour Opposition was careful to dissociate itself from such unconstitutional pressures, it made no secret of its sympathy with the miners and sent the Union its 'good wishes and support in their campaign'.

On 4th February, 1974, the Prime Minister announced that there would be a general election on 28th February, and appealed to the N.U.M., in the light of this and his reference of the miners' claim to the Pay Board on the vexed question of 'relativity', to suspend industrial action — but to no avail. For many observers the central issue of the election was 'Who Governs Britain?', but, while a majority of the electorate voted for the Conservatives, Labour emerged as the strongest single Party and formed a minority Government. The most significant Cabinet appointment was undoubtedly that of the ultra-socialist Michael Foot in place of Reginald Prentice, who, as Shadow Secretary for Employment since 1972, had raised trade union ire on more than one occasion. For the first time, the Left Wing in a Labour Government and in the trade union movement had gained ascendancy, and whether for tactical or genuinely doctrinal reasons, or an amalgam of both, had formed a coalition, with the balance of power on the trade union side.

The miners' strike was immediately settled, almost as a formality, and the speedy repeal of the Industrial Relations Act was accorded the highest priority. The Industrial Court and the Pay Board were to be wound up, as was the Commission on Industrial Relations, the rump of whose functions was to be transferred to a Conciliation and Arbitration Service. Statutory price control was to be continued. The enabling measures did not pass wholly unscathed through Parliament, despite a fragmented Opposition; the provision for re-funding tax paid by unions unregistered under the Industrial Relations Act was blocked, as was the restoration of the 'closed shop', but only temporarily. The T.U.C. issued its own guide-lines for free collective bargaining in a document entitled 'Collective Bargaining and the Social Contract.' Another general election quickly followed, in October, and this time Labour, with the 'social contract' at the heart' of its manifesto, gained a narrow over-all majority.

One of the principal architects of Labour's programme was Jack Jones of the Transport and General Workers'. Not so long before, on taking up office, he had derided T.U.C. generalship as 'Woodcockism', i.e., 'sacrificing trade union effectiveness at the point where it was most powerful — the place of work — in order to facilitate it operating where it was least influential, in talks with ministers'.[27]

In 1975 the Employment Protection Act finally fulfilled the pledges given to the T.U.C. by the Labour Party two years before. Michael Foot, the Secretary for Employment, was reported to have likened it to the repeal of the Combination Law in 1825; in fact, it was much more significant. It set up a new legal framework for industrial relations, stripped of any suggestion of compulsion for the trade unions. The sole and simple criterion for registration was proof of 'independence'. The Advisory Conciliation and Arbitration Service was to be put on a statutory footing, a Central Arbitration Committee was to replace the Industrial Arbitration Board, and there was to be an Employment Appeal Tribunal for the interpretation of points of law. There was, however, a whole battery of mandatory obligations on employers, including disclosure of information, guaranteed weekly wages, trade union recognition, maternity benefits and other contractual rights, with recourse to legal sanctions as necessary. One further claim sponsored by the T.U.C., although unions were by no means unanimous on it,[28] was for direct union participation in management; this was referred to a committee of inquiry under Lord Bullock.

The rout of the advocates of compulsion so far as the trade unions were concerned appeared complete. In practice, however, the 'social contract, — an astutely chosen term with a noble, if theoretical, ancestry — proved something of a delusion. It sought to give legitimacy to the wages free-for-all which the abrupt termination of a statutory policy, in the midst of an inflationary situation, made inevitable. It was a bipartite and far from specific understanding between the T.U.C. and the Labour Government, which purported to relate wage increases to the cost of living. Within the year, the rate of wage escalation soared to horrific heights of over 30 per cent, as one section emulated the success of another. It very quickly became apparent that the economy could not

stand a rate of inflation, on the Government's own estimates,
which was running far ahead of those of its trading com-
petitors. In July, 1975, the Government, with the reluctant
acquiescence of the T.U.C., re-introduced a wages policy,
none the less compulsory, despite the protestations of the
Secretary for Employment, because the sanctions were directed
only against erring employers, in both public and private
sectors.[29] It was in a crude form, a flat maximum (or, as the
T.U.C. insisted, an entitlement) of £6 a week, which was said
to be the formula of Jack Jones and certainly was in keeping
with the philosophy of the 'general' unions. A Government
publicity sheet acknowledged that it was 'rough justice', but
explained that 'until pay restraint begins to act on prices . . .
prices will go up faster than wages'. The impact was cushioned
by subsidies, but these were to be phased out in the public
sector and economic realism was to apply, apart from rescue
operations of large, labour-intensive — and strife-ridden —
enterprises, especially in the motor-manufacturing industry,
to mitigate levels of unemployment unprecedented since the
War. The long dilemma of reconciling the paramount need
for state direction in vital areas of the economy with the free
exercise of trade union power had not been resolved.

In less than a decade, the relationship between the State and
the trade unions had undergone a traumatic metamorphosis,
but it had not yet achieved stability. The violence of trade
union reaction had halted, and indeed reversed, the pressure
for institutional and procedural reform which had been
building up ever since the War and which the Commission
on Industrial Relations had been designed to promote. The
attempt even to prescribe standards of behaviour for trade
unions, in the public and private interest, had been totally
abandoned. Yet, paradoxically, the T.U.C.'s success had in
some ways diminished the status of the trade unions. The
scope of collective bargaining had contracted as the state
had taken responsibility, especially under the Employment

Protection Act, for imposing fresh obligations on the employers; the unions had become under it little more than
activating agents. They might find new outlets, again through
state intervention, in direct involvement in the business of
management, but to that extent they must acquire a duality
of responsibility which must weaken their relationship with
their constituents. They were now so closely associated with
Government policy that in no small measure they had become
part of the apparatus of the State; this must weaken the independence of government and of party which had been an
integral element of T.U.C. philosophy ever since its foundation
and which gave it much of its strength. At the same time, the
stand which the leadership of the T.U.C. had taken in the
last few years and which appeared to have been vindicated
by events — that the movement was not only quasi-political
but "party political" — could not be sustained indefinitely.
In the first place it was becoming clear that such a doctrine
did not command the support of the mass of the trade unionists, a large and increasing proportion of whom were 'white-
collar' workers. It was based on a style of leadership which
already, and probably as a reaction to recent events, was
being demonstrably, in union elections, tempered by a swing
towards moderation.[30] It also implied a unity of thought and
action which was lacking in the British trade union movement.
Finally, it was untenable in a democracy based on the British
party system. As it was, there were suggestions that the
perhaps over-close identification of the T.U.C. with Government had ominous undertones of the corporate state.

REFERENCES

1. MARTIN HARRISON: *Trade Unions and the Labour Party Since 1945* (Allen
   & Unwin, 1960), Chapter IV and Conclusion.
2. LEWIS MINKIN: 'The British Labour Party and the Trade Unions:
   Crisis and Compact' (*Industrial and Labor Relations Review*, Vol. 28,
   No. 1, Oct, 1974) pp. 15 ff.
3. *The Times*, 20th June, 1960.
4. V. L. ALLEN: *Trade Unions and the Government* (Longmans, 1960); *The
   Times Literary Supplement*, 21st October, 1960.

5. C. A. R. CROSLAND: *The Future of Socialism* (Jonathan Cape, 1956).
6. *Ibid.*, pp. 446–8;
    W. N. MEDLICOTT: *Contemporary England, 1914–1964* (Longmans, 1967), pp. 563, 579–89;
    ANDREW SHONFIELD: *British Economic Policy Since the War* (Penguin Books, 1959).
7. *Cmnd.* 7321.
8. *Cmnd.* 1628.
9. *Cmnd.* 1844.
10. *The Times*, 14th July, 1962.
11. *Machinery of Prices and Incomes Policy (Cmnd.* 2577);
    Prices and Incomes Policy (Cmnd. 2639);
    Prices and Incomes Policy: an 'Early Warning System' (Cmnd. 2808);
    Prices and Incomes Standstill (Cmnd. 3073);
    Prices and Incomes Standstill: Period of Severe Restraint (Cmnd. 3150).
12. House of Commons, 20th June, 1966.
13. *Report of Royal Commission on Trade Unions and Employers Organisations* (1968), ('Donovan Report'), *Cmnd.* 3628, paras. 362–81;
    In Place of Strife (1969), *Cmnd.* 3888, App. 2;
    ERIC WIGHAM: *Strikes and the Government 1893–1974* (Macmillan, 1976).
14. *House of Commons*, 20th June, 1966.
15. *Donovan Report*, paras. 161, 1018.
16. *Op. cit.*
17. House of Commons, 17th April, 1969.
18. ROBERT CARR, Shadow Secretary for Employment, House of Commons, 3rd July, 1969.
19. THOMAS BALOGH: *Labour and Inflation* (Fabian Society, 1970).
20. See p. 153.
21. Minister of State, Department of Employment, House of Commons, 23rd March, 1972.
22. *The Times Law Reports*, 27th and 28th July, 1972.
23. *A Programme for Controlling Inflation: The First Stage (Cmnd.* 5125), and the *Counter-Inflation (Temporary Provisions) Act*, 1972;
    The Programme for Controlling Inflation: The Second Stage (Cmnd. 5205), and the *Counter-Inflation Act*, 1973;
    Consultative Document on the Price and Pay Code (Cmnd. 5444) 1973.
24. *The Economist*, 22nd November, 1975.
25. Prime Minister, House of Commons, 9th January, 1974.
26. M. McGAHEY, 27th January, 1974. For a detailed interpretation of events see *The Fall of Edward Heath* (*Sunday Times* pamphlet, 1976).
27. Quoted MINKIN, *op. cit.*, p. 24.
28. See *The Structure of the Electricity Supply Industry in England and Wales: Report of the Committee of Inquiry (Cmnd.* 6388) 1976.
29. *The Attack on Inflation* (Cmnd. 6151).
30. *The Economist*, 10th January, 1976.

INDEX